D1612747

THE POPULATION OF CYPRUS

UNIVERSITY OF LONDON
INSTITUTE OF COMMONWEALTH STUDIES

✳

COMMONWEALTH PAPERS

General Editor

PROFESSOR W. H. MORRIS-JONES

23

THE POPULATION OF CYPRUS

Demographic Trends and
Socio-economic Influences

THE POPULATION OF CYPRUS

*

Demographic Trends and
Socio-economic Influences

BY

L. W. ST JOHN-JONES

PUBLISHED FOR THE
INSTITUTE OF COMMONWEALTH STUDIES
BY MAURICE TEMPLE SMITH

First published in Great Britain 1983
by Maurice Temple Smith Limited
Jubilee House, Chapel Road
Hounslow Middlesex TW3 1TX

British Library Cataloguing in Publication Data

St John-Jones, L. W.
 The population of Cyprus – (Commonwealth studies; 23)
 1. Cyprus – Population
 I. Title   II. Series
 304.6'095645

 ISBN 0-85117-232-6

Printed and bound in Great Britain at
The Camelot Press Ltd, Southampton

CONTENTS

FIGURES

FOREWORD

As subjects for books, small countries seldom excite the interest of publishers. This is understandable enough in terms of the size of market they offer but it is also unfortunate because studies of such countries can often be exceptionally rewarding. Size itself is admittedly an important variable and it would be rash to generalise from findings of such studies, but at the same time smallness makes for manageable projects with results which can frequently have wider and more general significance. Moreover, as we have been learning of late, small, even tiny, territories – such as the residual fragments of colonial empire – have the capacity to become substantial foci of international conflict.

The Institute of Commonwealth Studies has in its seminars frequently given consideration to small countries and mini-states and indeed one such set of papers, published many years ago (*Problems of Smaller Territories*, Athlone Press 1967), may be said to have drawn attention to their distinctive significance. In sponsoring work on the demography of Cyprus, the Institute had in mind its established concern with this field. At the same time it appeared that Cyprus was deserving of more scholarly attention by virtue not only of its continuing position as a problem of international dimensions but also of its considerable intrinsic interest. The present study of one especially important aspect of its development is a valuable contribution to a better understanding of this Mediterranean island.

W. H. MORRIS-JONES

ACKNOWLEDGMENTS

THIS study has been made possible by a grant to the Institute of Commonwealth Studies, University of London, from the Social Science Research Council. I record with appreciation my debt to both organisations.

In London, I have received valuable advice from Dr John Blacker of the London School of Hygiene and Tropical Medicine and Professor W. H. Morris-Jones and Mr T. E. Smith, Director and former Secretary respectively of the Institute of Commonwealth Studies. On both sides of the 'Green Line' in Cyprus so many people, officials and private individuals, have willingly and patiently discussed the data and their background with me that to list them all is impracticable and to mention only a few invidious. One exception must be Dr Theodore Papadopoullos, until recently the Director of the Cyprus Research Centre, whose expert advice on Cypriot history has been particularly helpful. To all of them I am most grateful. However, for the detail which the study contains, of both demographic analysis and general comment, I alone am responsible.

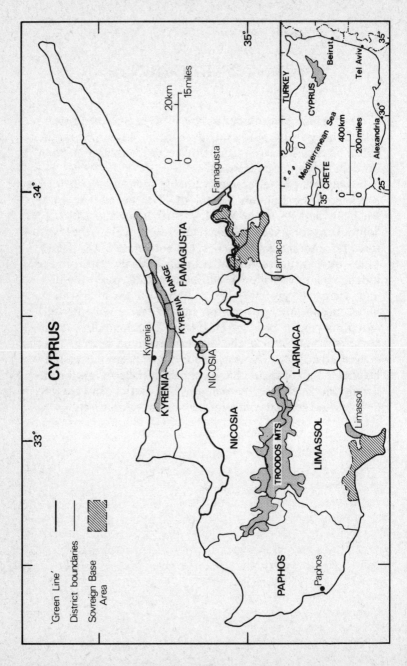

CYPRUS

1

THE GEOGRAPHICAL AND HISTORICAL BACKGROUND

Geography

CYPRUS lies in what is today an isolated corner of the Mediterranean, some sixty miles from the Syrian coast and about forty from Turkey. To the south there are 230 miles of sea to be crossed before Egypt, and to the west 200 miles until the nearest islands, Crete and those of the Aegean Sea, are reached. Cyprus lies on the 35th parallel north of the equator – the level, roughly, of Los Angeles and of Japan below Tokyo. Comprising 3,572 square miles, the island is large by Mediterranean standards, and is exceeded in size only by Sicily and Sardinia. Beside its neighbours, however, it is tiny, Turkey having something like eighty times its area and Egypt a hundred times, while to the east other Arab countries stretch for many hundreds of miles. The island's size is half of that of New Jersey in the United States and considerably smaller than Yorkshire in England. Shaped roughly like a stretched-out animal's skin, with the tail pointing north-east into the angle of the Mediterranean where Turkey and Syria meet, the island has a remarkable variety of physical characteristics. Close to, and parallel with, the north shore is the Kyrenia range of mountains, abrupt on the north side, spectacular from all angles, and rising at its highest point to 3,557 feet. This peak is no more than two and a half miles from the sea. In general the coastal plain is only a little wider and, being well watered from the mountains, is highly fertile. South of the Kyrenia range is the Mesaoria plain, comprising some 600 square miles, fertile in winter but parched in summer. Much of the remainder of the island is mountainous, not in a distinguishable ridge or series of peaks, but in a confusion of foothills leading up to the mountains, many of them steep, often interspersed with deep, inhabited valleys, and culminating in a central mass capped by Mount Troodos, 6,401 feet high. As the crow flies, Troodos is no more than fifteen miles from the sea either to the north or to the south and only thirty to the east, so here also are contrasts of vegetation, scenery, and life-style within short distances. The coasts are unbroken by natural harbours. From the mountains torrents rush down to the sea after every rainfall, but in the summer even the two main rivers are dry; none is navigable at any time.

Cyprus' climate varies greatly with the topography. Overall, the summer is dry and hot; in December, January, and February the rain can be heavy, but sunshine is still plentiful; in the months between the seasons the days are mild and the nights cool, and rain falls, but not often. Inland, in Nicosia for instance, the average maximum temperature in July and August is about 97°F, while at the end of the year it is nearer 60°, and frosts occur at night; on the coasts the maximum in summer is eight or nine degrees less, and in winter a degree or so higher, than on the central plain. Rainfall in Nicosia amounts to some fourteen inches a year, with slightly higher amounts on the coasts. In the mountains, on the other hand, temperatures are lower and rainfall is greater, and at Troodos skiing is a favourite sport in winter.

Four of the five main towns, Famagusta, Larnaca, Limassol, and Paphos, lie on the coast, not in natural harbours, but at points where landings could be made across the beaches. The capital, Nicosia, is situated in the Mesaoria plain, close to the pass leading over the northern range to Kyrenia. The first three towns are seaports, while the small harbour of Paphos is used for local trade and fishing. These towns, together with Kyrenia, are the headquarters of the six administrative districts, each of which bears the same name as the town. Rural settlements are seldom situated on the shore, probably because almost all are old, and in earlier centuries piracy and invasion were to be feared. Here, topography and character are linked, perhaps. Cypriots have been landsmen for generations, Christodoulou observes, and the sea rarely enters their lives or their literature; until this century most of them, perhaps, lived their lives out without ever setting eyes on it.[1]

History

For centuries of its early history, Cyprus lay close to the political centre of the world, and being small, strategically sited, and economically valuable, was invaded, fought over, and divided, owing its allegiance here and there, sometimes willingly but more often not. A greater contrast than its comparative isolation today from the mainstream of world events is difficult to imagine. The change was brought about, in general terms, by the shifting westwards of political power, the new routes and trends of trade following on the discovery of the Cape route to the Far East and of America, and finally by the Turkish conquest; it occurred, that is to say, in the fifteenth and sixteenth centuries.

An early landmark in Cypriot history was an Egyptian invasion in the fifteenth century B C. What kind of inhabitants the invaders found is uncertain, but some evidence suggests that they were of Aryan origin and had come from Phrygia or thereabouts. In time, Egyptian power was overtaken by that of Phoenicia, who, it is thought, founded a colony at Citium – the Chittim of the book of Genesis – near the present-day Larnaca. Various changes in the dominant power took place until Cyprus eventually became a part of the empire of the Macedonian Alexander the Great. After his death, it reverted to the rule of Egypt, or rather of the Ptolemies of Egypt, with their Greek origins and outlook. By now, Greek settlements existed in Cyprus and Greek influence was strong. In the last century B C the island passed under the rule of Rome. In A D 45, another landmark was reached – the conversion of the Roman pro-consul, followed no doubt by that of the people, to Christianity by St Paul, as related in the Acts of the Apostles. St Paul travelled with St Barnabas, himself a Cypriot, who was later martyred at Salamis near Famagusta, and it was on the discovery of St Barnabas' remains in the fifth century that the Byzantine emperor conferred independence on the Church of Cyprus and honours on its Archbishop, including the imperial prerogative of signing his name in red ink – a privilege still prized today. Cyprus passed to the Byzantine empire on the partition of the Roman empire in 395; later, it was occupied by Moslem Arabs for nearly a century and a half; and later still it returned again to Byzantine dominion.

Richard I of England came to Cyprus as the result of a storm at sea, and took the island in 1191 because his affianced bride and her vessels were rudely treated by the self-styled 'emperor' of the day. He was quickly succeeded by the Frankish Lusignan family whose three-hundred-year reign brought great prosperity: 'the wealth and luxury of its citizens, especially in the fourteenth century, evoked the amazement of all Western visitors. The rich merchants of Famagusta were wont, we are told, to give their daughters, on their marriage, jewels more precious *que toutes les parures de la reine de France*.' But Lusignan rule was feudal, and it became less powerful in Cyprus as the feudal system in general decayed. Its end came largely through rivalry with the Genoese and the Venetians: the former took Famagusta and retained it for a long period, and a Lusignan marriage with a Venetian lady led to a Venetian occupation in 1488. To the new rulers, Cyprus was little more than a military post confronting the Turkish empire; trade in the eastern Mediterranean was declining, and adminis-tration and agriculture were neglected. In consequence, the absorption of Cyprus into the Turkish realm after invasion in 1571 possibly imposed no greater hardships in the long run than those experienced in the previous century.

The Turkish occupation virtually removed Cyprus from con-tact with the developing world of the west. For Turkey also, Cyprus was an outpost of negative strategic value, being a potential danger in the hands of others. Profit was the objective of the administration, and the burden of taxation shaped the life of the country – incentive to hard work or thrift disappeared, villages were depopulated, people emigrated or were put to death in the attempt. The island 'gradually sank into a state of barren stagnation', to use the expression of one historian. But not all was bad. Serfdom disappeared, and the authority of the Orthodox Church was restored to the extent that it both acted as tax-gatherer and represented the people to their rulers. Turkish rule naturally ran the risk of opposition, and suspicion of Greek-Cypriot intentions came to a head in 1821. The govern-ment summoned the Archbishop and many notables to a meeting and, having trapped them, murdered almost all of them. Such occurrences, underlining the clear differentiation between Mos-lem rulers and Christian subjects, must have done much to concentrate the essentially Greek sentiments of the great majority of the population.

The administration, although not the legal possession, of the island passed to Britain in 1878 as part of a concerted effort against expanding Russian influence in the Near East. Despite having had no say in it, most Cypriots welcomed the change. For the Greeks, another goal now came into view, expressed by the Archbishop in addressing the first High Commissioner as he landed at Larnaca: '. . . we trust that Great Britain will help Cyprus, as it did the Ionian Islands, to be united with Mother Greece, with which it is nationally connected.' The new administration proceeded in the uneventful but orderly way of British colonial governments, giving its attention to popular representation, the administration of justice, tax reform, communications, agriculture, and forestry. Yet, expenditure was minimal; not only was the country poor, but some of its revenue had to be paid to Turkey in compensation for lost profits.[2] With the entry of Turkey into the First World War on the side of Germany, Cyprus was annexed by Britain. Material progress in the two following decades was slow, if steady, but in the 1940s a conjunction of several factors marked a take-off point in the island's history. Ideas and outlook became widened by a new awareness of world events – Cyprus was possibly next in line after Crete for invasion by the Axis powers – as British troops lived in Cyprus and Cypriots joined the allied forces overseas. Economically the island became better off, as the armed services spent money and provided jobs; purchasing power not only increased, but was more evenly spread than previously. In 1940 the Agricultural Debtors Relief Law did much to loose the age-old stranglehold of the money-lender on agriculture, and the post-war Programme of Development set out a comprehensive and practical guide to economic and social progress. A miracle of modern science eliminated malaria, the 'scourge of Cyprus', the incidence of tuberculosis fell, and so did infant mortality.

A sign of the new vitality came in the 1950s, when after talking of *enosis* (union with Greece) since 1878, the Greek community turned words to deeds with a campaign of violence against the government. Inevitably it took on racial overtones, because the Turkish community was hostile to all idea of rule by Greece. Many lives were lost in the terrorism of the years 1955–59, which boded badly for the inter-communal amity on which nationhood would depend.

Enosis was rejected, and independence came to Cyprus in August 1960, but the inter-communal stability brought about by constitutional checks and balances hardly survived the euphoria of the island's first non-dependent status since 1191. At the end of

1963 the two communities parted company, and ten years' confusion followed, marked by inter-communal clashes, the growing isolation of the Turkish community, and a second terrorist campaign aimed at *enosis*. The stalemate could not last. What broke it was a coup in mid-1974 against the government by its own national guard, engineered from Greece. Turkey landed troops on the island, claiming justification under the tripartite independence agreements, and after abortive negotiations, occupied some 40 per cent of the total area. Greeks were displaced from north to south and Turks in the opposite direction; everyday communication between the two sides ceased; the Turks declared a Turkish Federated State of Cyprus in 1975. Up to the time of writing, this dichotomy has continued, despite sporadic attempts at a settlement – unsatisfactory to both communities, and a threat to peace locally and in the region.

2

THE DEMOGRAPHIC INFORMATION AVAILABLE

Censuses

THE first of Cyprus' population censuses was taken in April 1881. £1,000 was allocated for the task, and the Sanitary Inspector, Dr F. W. Barry, was appointed to superintend it. Lists of villages were prepared, and were checked by the officer in charge of the survey of the island;[1] in the towns, streets were named and houses numbered. Enumerators, who were hard to find, were remunerated modestly, and honoraria were paid to *mukhtars* (village headmen) for their assistance. The census schedule, printed in English, Greek, and Arabic, asked about each person's name, relationship to the head of the family, sex, conjugal condition, age, place of birth, occupation, infirmities, religion, and mother tongue, and answers were given in a variety of languages – Greek, Turkish, Arabic, Armenian, Persian, and some European tongues. The form was to be filled in by the occupier, the General Instructions stated, adding that 'the facts will be published in General Abstracts only, and strict care will be taken that the returns are not used for the gratification of curiosity'.

The number of persons enumerated was 186,173. The Superintendent's report was brief – unfortunately, for an account of the field work might have helped to indicate its accuracy. Two observations which it contained are worth recalling, in the light of trends to be noted later. He ascribed the excess of males in the population to a majority of men among the 'various immigrants who have been attracted to the island during recent years', and he felt himself unable to judge – although he was a doctor of both medicine and science – the theory that, in Cyprus, mortality of females was higher than that of males; there was an instinctive disinclination on the part of the Mohammedans to give the correct number of the female population, but nevertheless the deficiency of females in the population was probably genuine.

15

The *Annual Report* observed that although the census was a complete novelty and was likely to be associated in people's minds with projects for new taxes, the information was given cheerfully, and the enumeration was a complete success. A century later, we may think that Cyprus owes a debt to Dr Barry for an example of careful and economic planning which was followed closely in later years.

That the 1891 census did so was stated by its Superintendent, F. G. Glossop, who reported that although the enumerator's wage failed to attract many 'of the better class of Cypriots', the field work was fairly satisfactory. Perhaps the main feature of this count to be noted was the repeated request that householders complete the census schedules themselves, the enumerator being available to take over when necessary. The brief reports on the 1901 and 1911 censuses, conducted by A. Mavrogordato, suggest that precedent was again followed exactly, except that in the latter year a question on literacy was added. 'It is generally admitted that the enumeration was carefully and accurately carried out', the 1901 report observed. The following two censuses, in 1921 and 1931, were also conducted by one man,[2] C. H. Hart Davis; the reports which he wrote were even more laconic than his predecessors', but there is little doubt that again precedent was followed very closely.

The next census, in November 1946, had a full-time director, D. A. Percival, used an elaborated questionnaire, and was based on a three-round procedure – an initial house-listing, a preliminary enumeration, and a final check on census day itself – all in keeping with increasing prosperity and a forward-looking mood. Again, enumerators were not easy to find, but in the report they were credited with public spirit and 'painstaking and excellent work', while the response of the public was said to be excellent. New questions concerned nationality, level of education, knowledge of the English language, duration of marriage, the numbers of children born and surviving to women who were, or had been, married, secondary (in addition to principal) occupation, and agricultural holdings. The tradition of self-enumeration was partly maintained, but to what extent it was used is uncertain. The Superintendent's report was a landmark not only in Cyprus' demographic statistics but in its literature generally, reviewing, as it did, past data, commenting on and analysing most of the census topics, and projecting the size of the population in the future.[3] Outside Cyprus, experts quickly recognised its merit, for instance the Regional Statistician of the United Nations Food and Agriculture Organisation, who observed: 'I think it is the best census report for a small country that I have ever seen.'

Little information about the conduct of the 1960 census is available. It was directed by the full-time Statistical Officer, S. Vassiliou; the three-round procedure was repeated; and the instructions were detailed – and pithy, as when enumerators were told, 'Maintain a friendly manner, but don't waste time in small talk.' The questionnaire, on the other hand, was anything but concise, containing thirty-three numbered questions about population topics, some of which were sub-divided into further questions, plus thirty on housing; and one question alone, on level of education, was accompanied by fifty-three boxes denoting different types of schools and varying levels within them, of which only one was to be selected and ticked. Whether the tradition of self-enumeration, specifically allowed by the instructions, was actually practised is not known now, but it seems unlikely. The report was limited to tabular material, and even so omitted the results of several of the census questions.

Two subsequent counts of the non-Turkish population were made, in 1973 and 1976. The latter was originally designed as a registration of property lost in the 1974 war. In neither case has a report been issued, but a number of tables have appeared in the annual *Demographic Report*, showing populations purporting to be those of the whole island but being actually the enumerated non-Turkish populations grossed up on the basis of the racial division of the population in 1960, plus, in the case of 1973 at least, known migratory movements after that date. Post-enumeration surveys estimated undercounts of 2·2 and 1·2 per cent respectively.

How accurate have these censuses been? While some indications will be given later through analysis of their results, study of the conditions and methodology of an enumeration – or, better, a series of enumerations – often suggests some ideas of reliability, not in mathematical terms but rather on a comparative basis. Beginning thus, a census producing an error of 10 per cent in the enumerated population may be considered of poor quality; an efficient census will often result in one of, perhaps, 3 per cent or less. The quality of a census is often level throughout its various stages, because in all but the most elaborate organisations, the hallmark of one man, the director, is imprinted on them all. Certainly, factors such as budget restrictions can have their effect, but they are often recognisable in retrospect. Examination of the censuses' methods does, then, suggest some implications about accuracy.

Cyprus' first census undoubtedly set a good precedent, for its time, of planning and economy. While officials might be excused for not knowing every corner of their districts, so new was British rule, they had the assistance of an outstanding survey team, and the *mukhtars*, the village authorities, were a paid part of the field organisation. The population counted was no more than 186,000. In a *de facto* census, taken without exceptional circumstance such as food rationing, an overcount may be ruled out. At the same time, it is quite possible that in a small population living in well-defined agglomerations, virtually no household was omitted. Expenditure was not lavish, but on the other hand the Superintendent did not report inadequacy of funds; travel among the mountain villages must have been difficult – yet wherever anyone travelled and lived, enumerators and *mukhtars* could travel too, because they were local people. Even if every household were located, individual members might have been omitted – but the sex ratio was found to be 1,037 males per 1,000 females, a figure which does not suggest that many females were overlooked; nor is there any sign that young children were omitted either. Slightly higher ratios of men were found in the towns than in the villages – a perfectly rational result. All that is known about the census suggests the likelihood of a very accurate count by any standard.

Much the same may be said of the succeeding five enumerations. Usually, census practice improves with experience, but in Cyprus this process could easily have been countered by factors such as shortage of funds or the inability of a part-time Superintendent to give all the attention needed to an additional job. As will be seen later, it seems possible that the 1931 enumeration actually fell a little below earlier standards. In general, however, accuracy could well have been at a high level from 1881 to 1931.

In 1946, much improved organisation and a far larger budget

gave the essential basis for a count of very good quality. Planning and execution were clearly carried out with meticulous care. The public cooperated well, just as it always had. All in all, the conditions for an accurate enumeration were exceptionally good – better than ever before or after. The Superintendent has told the author that in the following years no suspicion of a significant undercount was ever raised.

The repeated use in 1960 of the three-round procedure again laid the base for an exceptionally accurate count. However, no information about financial provision is available, and although the recent achievement of independence may well have created a general atmosphere of cooperation with the government, the political disturbances of the 1950s could have given rise to contrary feelings in some quarters. In Cyprus it remains the impression that the count was of good quality.

From 1881 to 1960, therefore, we may think that the censuses gave data of above-average quality, and that Cyprus was more fortunate in this respect than the great majority of developing countries. As for 1973 and 1976, the questions asked in the enumerations were few, and no information other than the results of the post-enumeration surveys already mentioned is available to indicate how good the results may have been.

Registration of births and deaths

Totals of the births and deaths registered annually, after appearing for certain years in the mid-1880s, have been published regularly since 1901, and figures of infant deaths since 1916. Births were classified by sex for the first time in 1947, and deaths in 1948. Two years later, the age of the mother and the age of the deceased were added. From 1951 to 1963 births were cross-classified by religion – Greek Orthodox, Moslem, Armenian-Gregorian, and Other; deaths were similarly classified from 1951 to 1962, and infant deaths from 1951 to 1957.

Registration was the responsibility of the *mukhtars*, who compiled register sheets, and sent them each month to the District Commissioner. A copy went to the Director of Medical Services, who collated them for the island up to the 1950s. The system then broke down, the 1955 issue of *Vital and Migration Statistics* stating that as a large proportion of the *mukhtars* had resigned owing to intimidation by Eoka (a Greek-Cypriot political organisation), registration was incomplete. The numbers actually registered continued to be published up to 1963 (1961 in the case of infant deaths), and at the same time estimates were also given, based on the trends of the three years preceding 1955. Examples were:

	Reported		Estimated	
	Births	Deaths	Births	Deaths
1955	12,849	2,608	13,747	3,024
1958	5,738	621	14,320	3,450
1961	10,429	1,540	14,934	3,254

By 1961, it might be thought, registration would have been reasonably complete again, but clearly this was not the case. The *Demographic Report* did not suggest any reason why it remained deficient. At other points, too, more information might have been expected, for instance some explanation of the following unlikely series of infant deaths:

	Reported	Estimated
1953	633	–
1954	722	–
1955	380	433
1956	177	440
1957	162	435

If this series was implausible, then later estimates were too, for instance 433 in 1960, and with them the claim of *Vital and Migration Statistics 1962* that Cyprus had some of the lowest death and infant mortality rates in the world.

From 1964 the parting of the Greek and Turkish communities added a further complication – the need to guess the numbers of vital events among the Turks before adding them on to those estimated for the non-Turkish population. How this was done was not explained. In 1964, for instance, the *Demographic*

Report estimated 14,200 live births and 3,900 deaths, but did not mention the absence of Turkish returns and the consequent requirement of grossing up the first estimates to include the Turkish population before island-wide estimates could be published. The comment it did make was in the following terms: 'Because of the anomalous political situation prevailing in the island in 1964, under-registration of births and deaths was more acute, and as a result, some tables of births and deaths were omitted from this year's report'; and in 1968 it stated: 'In the absence of a fully articulated registration system, all data on births and deaths given in this report are estimates based on past trends, i.e. it has been assumed that the birth and death rates have been rather constant since 1960.'

Subsequently some revisions of the published totals were made. An enquiry in 1971 of hospitals, clinics, and cemeteries, it was reported, resulted in findings about the numbers of births and deaths which were probably reasonably accurate, so the published figures for the years 1966 to 1971 were revised. Then, following on the 1973 census of the non-Turkish population, the *Demographic Report* (1973) stated that matching the census results with the registration data showed that deaths had been greatly under-recorded while births had been overestimated, so the estimates of both had been revised back to 1961. The following, for instance, were the figures first issued, and then revised in 1973, for the year 1966:

Births 14,810   Deaths 3,513
revised 13,250   revised 5,991

The data for 1966–71 had now been revised twice. Next, after the 1976 count of the government-controlled area, the estimates of vital events since 1974 were amended; and in 1978, new calculations indicated that births since 1971 had been overestimated by 12–14 per cent. Some care is therefore required in picking out the latest revisions in issues of the *Demographic Report* since 1964.

From 1977 the Turkish-Cypriot authorities have published totals of vital registrations.[4] In the absence of information on the methods of assembling them, it is not possible to assess their likely accuracy beyond saying that the numbers of deaths given are implausibly low.

21

Migration

From 1920 the numbers of persons arriving at, and leaving, the main ports and, later, the airport have been recorded, and annual figures, entitled 'net migration', obtained by differencing the two totals, issued. Net migration was usually negative, signifying an excess of departures over arrivals: −822 persons in the first year, for instance, −2,793 in 1924, generally smaller figures for the next twenty years, and numbers around −2,000 or −3,000 again in the early 1950s. This series of data continued up to 1966.

Beginning in 1955, another series appeared – the numbers of immigrants and emigrants, in contradistinction to arrivals and departures. Nevertheless, the official figures of 'net migration' continued to derive from the latter. As it is arguable that the difference between the numbers of immigrants and emigrants properly constitutes net migration, it is of interest to see whether the two methods of calculation gave divergent results. Both series are available for the years 1955 to 1966. In those twelve years, official net migration was −58,861; calculated by differencing immigration and emigration, it was −65,190. A margin of 10 per cent between the two figures may seem insignificant in a branch of data collection which is notorious for its problems, but examination of individual years suggests that the comparison is not straightforward. Some examples follow:

	Official net migration	Immigrants minus emigrants
1955	− 3,102	− 5,359
1956	− 3.853	− 1,335
1958	− 6,072	− 3,862
1961	− 7,316	−12,316
1964	−12,571	− 4,814

Excesses occur sometimes in the official series, sometimes in the other, with no pattern to help explain them. Do the backgrounds to both series serve to indicate their reliability?

Because Cyprus is an island, counting persons arriving and leaving should not be difficult. However, relative to the population, the figures in question are large, so a small error in the recording process results in a number which is large in the context of net migration. Quite different factors govern the reliability of the other series – the *intention* of the individual and his willingness to declare it. As regards immigrants, foreigners immigrating and taking up jobs can be traced today, if not on entering, then at the stage of obtaining a work permit; but few of the immigrants, probably, are foreigners. *Tourism, Migration and Travel Statisitics*[5] stated in 1973 that no reliable data on immigration existed. As for emigrants, nothing compels them to state their intention of emigrating. In 1974, the same report stated that the recorded number of emigrants was believed to be less than the true figure, and that an unknown number of permanent residents who left after July for business, holiday, or other reasons had in fact emigrated or found temporary employment in other countries. The remark applied to an exceptional year, but it could be true of other years as well.

In 1976 a different series of annual figures entitled 'net migration' was issued, going back to 1960. Some of its totals differ radically from those published earlier, and it is easy to guess from those of two of the years cited above (– 13,296 in 1961, and – 5,040 in 1964) that their base is the numbers of immigrants and emigrants, not arrivals and departures. However, they do not exactly match any previously published figures, and towards the end of the series they must have used unpublished data. For example, net migration in 1973 is given as +1,808. As emigrants in that year totalled 1,312, immigrants must have been put at 1,808 + 1,312 = 3,120, a figure not mentioned elsewhere.

Although the *numbers* of emigrants may well have been understated since 1955, data on an exceptionally wide range of characteristics have been given – on their sex, age, race, occupational group, district of residence, and destination. Unless the possible understatement of total numbers has been selective – which seems unlikely – the patterns of these data should be generally reliable.

Reference is sometimes found to the numbers of Cypriots resident abroad, for instance in the 1964 *Demographic Report,* which stated that enquiry had been made of the Statistical Offices of all countries to determine the numbers of Cypriots living there. Sixty answers had been received, of which most said the information was not available, but others had given apparently exact figures, such as the United Kingdom – 41,898; Australia – 9,732; Greece – 2,284; Lebanon – 825; in all, 55,365. This total must have been disappointing, for today it is commonly said in Cyprus that Cypriots in the United Kingdom alone number between 110,000 and 150,000. Such figures include not only first-generation Cypriots, but second, and possibly later, generations too, and therefore have little statistical significance, but as the 1971 census of Great Britain recorded 73,000 persons born in Cyprus, a total of well over 100,000 persons of clearly Cypriot origin in Britain today is not unlikely. A new total of persons actually born in Cyprus will be available shortly from Britain's 1981 census.

The published migration data included Turkish-Cypriots up to July 1974, for they continued to be counted at the ports and the airport, all of which were under control of the government. Since July 1974, the government's data have excluded all movements at the Turkish-controlled ports and airport.

3

POPULATION GROWTH BEFORE 1878

THE population counted by the first British census proceeded to double in just over fifty years. Had it experienced similar growth in the past, it would have totalled some 90,000 around 1820 and 45,000 in 1770. In the seventeenth century the island would have been virtually uninhabited. Yet Cyprus' history makes it clear that this was not the case. A radical change in the pattern of growth therefore occurred at some time.

Various factors which influence such changes should be kept in mind. Disease was rife, it goes without saying – plague and other epidemics swept the island from time to time, and malaria was endemic. Droughts occurred regularly, severe earthquakes were not infrequent, and crops were wiped out by locusts. Yet all these risks were present in other countries too, so there were other, special, factors to affect population growth in Cyprus. Foremost among them, perhaps, was the small size of the island and its people; an epidemic or an earthquake must have had comparatively very large consequences. Even the locusts were subject to this factor – in many countries they came from, and retreated to, neighbouring deserts and waste lands, but the Cyprus breed was indigenous, and the small cultivated area of the island was its total prey. A turbulent history must have taken its toll; for instance, it was recorded that more than 14,000 people died on the day in 1570 when the Turks took Nicosia – some 7 per cent of the population. Perhaps the most significant factor of all was the ease with which people could come to, or leave, the island. It meant that significant numbers could disappear, or return, almost overnight; and the violence of invaders, the oppression of rulers, the recurring incidence of famine and epidemic meant that they probably did, and on a far larger scale than the remarkable 2½ per cent of the population reported to have emigrated in 1960. This is not to suggest that uprooting one's home was easy; rather that when circumstances are hard enough, any possibility is grasped. For many, emigrating by sea was probably simpler than journeying across the island; and for three centuries Cyprus was a province of Turkey, so except for the local loss of tax revenue, movement to another province was probably not of much consequence. In the same way, incentive and ease of movement have continued to prompt emigration from Cyprus up to the present.

Since the size of the population before 1878 clearly cannot be derived from a basis of regular growth, any idea of trends requires an examination of the counts and estimates made at different times.

The reign of the Ptolemies in the last two centuries BC was prosperous, and was long enough for a considerable population to build up. Various opinions of its likely size have been formed. It was much greater than the 335,000 of 1928, the *Handbook of Cyprus* of that year thought, pointing to evidence such as the reputed capacity of the aqueduct bringing water to the capital, Salamis – enough to supply 120,000 people. Fertile and mountainous Cyprus must have been attractive to the people of nearby arid countries, but while a comparatively large population was likely, its number must have been limited by the island's productive capacity. Alastos has calculated that if the crops produced the same yield as in the 1950s – which seems unlikely – between 400,000 and half a million people could have been fed.[1] Almost certainly the population did not reach that level, and it could perhaps have found its limit at about 300,000.

In succeeding centuries it decreased, probably attaining a low figure about the time of the Arab occupation, and increasing again thereafter. Little further evidence is available before Venetian times, when, from counts and observations, it seems to have numbered between 100,000 and 200,000. But in the prosperous days of Lusignan rule it had been bigger, and a total of half a million has again been mentioned. However, some experts have reservations about that figure, the Conservator of Forests of the 1950s observing, for instance: 'Judging from the ruined village sites I have seen in the mountains and the foothills, the population in the fourteenth century cannot have been as great as 400,000. Most of the ruined settlements of that period are very small and poor in construction.'[2] Twice, then – once towards the end of the pre-Christian era, and once in the fourteenth century – stable and efficient government allowed the population to swell to about the maximum the island could sustain. That maximum was possibly in the region of 300,000 persons.

Under Venice, the total was apparently less than half that of two hundred years previously. No doubt some people emigrated, and there were reports that outbreaks of plague in 1348 and 1470 carried off a half and three-tenths of the population respectively. The towns were unsanitary and undernourishment was common, we read; and a traveller observed of Famagusta under the Genoese that men died in great numbers, and 'I remained in the city in great fear.'[3] In 1490 a delegation to Venice mentioned a total of 106,000, while a count by the administration in the next year found 168,000 persons. At the outset of the period in which some detailed figures began to appear, a problem about their reliability is thus seen immediately. It was complicated by the method of enumerating taxpayers or householders, not individuals. The small numbers must have caused concern, for at one point the island got Venice to agree that immigrants be offered inducements such as exemption from salt tax for twenty-five years.

There is a notable discrepancy between the 200,000 persons estimated in about 1570 and the count by the Turks in 1571–72 which resulted in 85,000 Christian taxpayers aged 14 to 50 plus dependants – a total of 270,000, plus 20,000 Turks, or 290,000 in all, Percival calculated. At just over two dependants a taxpayer aged 14 to 50, this total seems low; it could well have been 375,000, reckoning on three, rather than two, dependants. Since some credence is generally given to the total of about 270,000, its likely value is worth examining. The Turks listed taxpayers rather than individuals. Archimandrite Kyprianos in his history of 1788 – the only report of the 'census' – stated that the Ottomans not only 'used the books and accounts of the Latin sovereigns to discover how much revenue the island yielded to the royal treasury, but examined certain unhappy Cypriots – they made known to the commission of enquiry and to the Pasha the revenues, estates, villages and even in detail the families in each village and their houses'. Whether totals of revenue and population obtained under virtual duress were exaggerated or understated cannot be known; the incentive for people to try to escape taxation is obvious, but there was, presumably, an equally strong

interest on the part of the authorities to overstate the tax potential
– and farm out the collection on that basis. And since property as
well as individuals was in question, was it possible that one
individual owning, or farming, more than one plot of land was
entered as many times? Clear uncertainty about the figures may
be seen in the Archimandrite's wording: 'Before the capture there
was a total population, as we learn from the historian Coronelli,
of 197,000 souls, so that we may accept the statement that after
the Turkish occupation 85,000 taxable males were entered on the
registers.' Unfortunately he offered no explanation of a large
population increase in two years characterised by an invasion and
'great and distressing dearth and famine, the result of war' –
conditions which left a state he described as 'the general captivity
and enslavement of such of the wretched Cypriots as survived'.
Kyprianos was, in fact, markedly vague about such detail, as we
see from his report of a 'census' taken in 1777, a year in which he
must have been writing his history; it recorded a considerable
majority of Moslems in the population, contrary to other counts
and estimates, and evoked his comment that many European
travellers doubted whether the Ottomans exceeded the Christians. If this historian could not state categorically whether one
group or the other was currently in a large majority, perhaps he
had good reason not to doubt openly the accuracy of his rulers'
'censuses' of either 1571–72 or 1777.

If the population under Venice reached 200,000, it could
hardly have increased to 290,00 or 370,000 immediately after the
Turkish invasion. As the population obviously declined subsequently, the Turkish, rather than the Venetian, figure may be
disregarded. What, then, *was* the population total in the early
Turkish days? The invasion took its toll in dead, it was reported;
doubtless it caused some Greeks as well as Venetians to leave the
island; altogether, perhaps, it caused a loss of 30–50,000
persons. The remaining Greeks, then, numbered 150–170,000;
there were also some Turks, 20,000 according to Kyprianos; so
the total numbered around 180,000. Admittedly an agent of the
Duke of Savoy estimated 250,000 in 1600, but as he appears to
have exaggerated the island's revenues,[4] he may have overstated
the population too.

Looking ahead, we may remember Hill's dictum in his *History
of Cyprus* that, after 1571, 'It would be rash, in view of the wide

28

divergence between the figures given by various sources, to hope for any trustworthy estimate of the total number of the population. Even the official records fail to carry conviction, when we remember the observation of Ali Bey that the government never succeeded in learning how many Greeks were in the island.'[5] Ali Bey – a Spaniard despite his name – writing of the early 1800s, related that the Porte sent a commissioner 'to make an exact enumeration of the Greek families, but he was "got at", loaded with gold, and went away with his task unfulfilled'. However, certain pointers to population levels can be found.

In the seventeenth century few estimates were made; of them, the following may be noted:

		Source
1641	107–120,000	Inspector of the Porte
1670	140–155,000	Barrie
1673	62–69,000	Osman Pasha
About 1673	180,000	Evliya
About 1693	126–140,000	Coronelli

All the estimates except that of Evliya were of taxpayers; those figures have been multiplied by three and a half or four to give the numbers of Christians, to which 20–30,000 Turks have been added to give the total population. Which estimates are the most credible? Neither Evliya nor Osman was in Cyprus; the Porte's inspector, on the other hand, came to the island to investigate local conditions, and, according to Kyprianos, he 'sought out and wrote down by name every *rayah*'. Barrie lived in Cyprus; and Coronelli was a historian of note. Omitting Evliya and Osman, the series suggests that from 1640 the population remained at about 120–140,000.

Kyprianos's account of conditions makes a decrease to 120–140,000 in the seventeenth century plausible. Taxes increased, he reported; the avarice of the pashas was insatiable; the island suffered from repeated droughts and from locusts; the plagues of 1641 and 1692 wasted and ruined the country. At other points he recorded that conditions reduced the Cypriots to such straits that many fled to the Syrian coasts and the island was growing deserted, while a visitor observed that the number of Cypriots could not be determined, as many of them removed every year on account of the prodigious taxes.

Even less information about the eighteenth century has been found. The most noteworthy estimates appear to be:

		Source
1738	63–72,000	Pococke
1745	56–64,000	Drummond
1760s	56–64,000	Mariti
1777	probably about 60,000	'Census'

Pococke and Drummond were among the first of those travellers whose estimates are sometimes quoted, along with figures from other sources such as the Turkish 'censuses', to form a series ending with the British total of 1881. Naturally a visitor could no more estimate the population by his own observation than today's tourist can; their estimates were, therefore, hearsay. The only value of such estimates lies in the remote possibility that they were taken from reliable sources unknown to us.

In calculating the above totals, the ratio of three and a half to four dependants per taxpayer has again been used. Drummond actually recorded totals of 150,000 Turks and 50,000 Christians, figures so obviously incorrect that new totals have been calculated from his 12,000 Greek and 4,000 Turkish taxpayers. The 'census' of 1777 recorded 10,487 taxpayers and 84,000 persons, but as Papadopoullos has discovered, the latter figure was an estimate added by an unknown person eleven years later; the population total given here has, therefore, also been calculated from the number of taxpapers.

As all the totals are based on the number of taxpayers – which varied from 10,487 to 12,000 – it is not surprising that the population appeared to fluctuate but little. But did the population really halve between the late seventeenth century and 1750? Historians tend to believe that it reached a nadir at the latter period. Hill, for instance, thought the condition of the island deplorable – mortality was high, people were emigrating to escape taxes, crops were scanty, trade was trifling. Even so, there must be doubt about the tax lists themselves. We may be sure that they were evaded when possible, and since they were controlled by the Orthodox Church, evasion was probably well organised. It was just at that time that Ali Bey wrote that the government never succeeded in learning how many Greeks there were, adding that they owned to a total of 32,000, but that well-informed sources raised that number to 100,000. Nevertheless, the population did decrease from the seventeenth century, according to every indication.

The picture is further confused by two statements that the Moslems considerably outnumbered the Christians, one, already noted, by Kyprianos, and the other by a British consul, de Vezin, the latter recording that the ratio was actually three to one. No explanation of such a claim is known, and as Kyprianos' attitude to his own figures appeared ambivalent, it seems safe to agree today with Luke in concluding 'with comparative safety that at no time were the Turks in Cyprus superior in number to the Christians'.

Many more totals[6] were reported for the nineteenth than for earlier centuries by visitors and foreign consuls, and also by a count, or a revision of the tax lists, by the governor in 1841, the results of which come to us through a traveller, Lacroix. Some of the totals follow:

		Source
1815	60–70,000	Turner
1829	73–84,000	French consul
1841	about 110,000	'Census', via Lacroix
1870s	144,000	Ritter
1881	186,000	British census

Others fit in less well with this pattern – for instance one of 100,000 in 1821, another of 25,000 in 1827, and yet another of 180,000 in 1858 – but those listed here are probably among the more reliable. Of the series, only the 1829 total has been grossed up from the number of taxpayers, and again multipliers of three and a half and four have been used.

All four totals were divided into Greeks and Turks in a ratio of two or two and a half to one. The exact figures of Ritter's – 100,000 Christians and 44,000 Moslems – are noteworthy, because his estimate was made within seven years of the first British census, when 45,458 Moslems were enumerated. In the

1870s, therefore, the number of Turks was known quite accurately; on the other hand the Christians were almost certainly underestimated by a third, 137,000 being found in 1881. The point supports the thesis that the Christian population was often, or consistently, underestimated under Turkish rule.

The totals imply that the population more than doubled between 1820 and 1881. Yet the executions of 1821 were followed by a long period of persecution, so that, according to an observer, the Greeks were forced into one of two alternatives, escaping from the island or embracing the faith of their persecutors, while they themselves wrote to the Russian consul that some had been reduced to flight, and that the boundless greed of the governors was the cause of the island's depopulation. So many left that attempts were made to entice them back. In 1830, for instance, the Archbishop begged the Cypriots in Cairo to return, with the promise of reduced taxation. This pattern of events does not fit that of population growth suggested by the estimates, and increases of 30 to 50 per cent between 1815 and 1829 and a further 30 per cent by 1840 are highly unlikely. Thereafter, conditions improved in certain ways, but it is hard to think that yet another 30 per cent was achieved by the 1870s.

There is evidence to suggest a population of some 160,000 Christians at the beginning of the Turkish regime and about 135,000 at the end. If such figures are approximately correct, the generally accepted decline over three hundred years was exaggerated. Within that period there are strong indications of some decrease which persisted throughout the seventeenth and eighteenth centuries, to be followed from 1830 or so by a mild recovery. The size of the Christian population probably fluctuated within short periods, as people migrated in consequence of epidemics, droughts and bursts of oppressive taxation. Nothing is known of the numbers migrating, but the accounts of the time tend to leave the reader surprised that any Christian population at all remained. That it did was probably due to periodic return migration, and even to the immigration of newcomers. All such movement must have been made in the light of conditions not only at home but at the destination as well. As the latter presumably included most of the factors which drove people out of Cyprus from time to time, migration should have occurred in both directions – insignificant in numbers to the Turkish empire, but important to Cyprus because of its small population. Whatever the overall growth or decline – and the latter seems more likely – of the population under Turkish rule was, it is not possible to distinguish between the contributions to it of natural increase, or lack of it, and emigration, but it would not be surprising if the lattter were an important factor.

A final point is of interest. Not only is the coincidence of the Venetian count of 168,000 persons, the estimate made here of some 180,000 persons about 1575, and the enumerated total of 186,000 in 1881 noteworthy, but the distribution of population among the six districts was almost identical in 1491 and 1881. Apparently the 400-year transition from medieval society through Moslem hegemony, from comparative affluence through political and economic stagnation, had in total as little effect on where people lived in Cyprus as on their number.

4

POPULATION GROWTH AFTER 1878

The total population

THE eight censuses of the whole country revealed the population increases seen in Table 1.

TABLE 1: THE GROWTH OF THE POPULATION, 1881–1960

Census of	Population	Percentage increase	Annual increase per cent
1881	186,173		1.18
1891	209,286	12·4	1·25
1901	237,022	13·3	1·46
1911	274,108	15·6	1·26
1921	310,715	13·4	1·14
1931	347,959	12·0	1·73
1946	450,114	29·4	1·74
1960	573,566	27·4	

Since it is not unlikely that the censuses up to 1921 resulted in small undercounts which generally decreased but never disappeared, the increases noted in that period may be slightly exaggerated. Further, there is a strong suspicion, enlarged on in the Appendix, of significant under-enumeration of young children in 1931 and possibly of some undercount of the remainder of the population too, so the recorded drop in the growth rate in the 1920s may have been illusory and the contrasting rate from 1931 to 1946 less remarkable than it appears to be. Data from the 1973 and 1976 'mini-censuses' of the non-Turkish-Cypriot population will be given later as part of the discussion of ethnic groups, but it may be noted now that the published total of 631,778 *de jure* for 1973 – grossed up from the enumerated population on the basis of the ethnic division of the population in 1960 – was probably

34

accurate enough for most practical purposes, even though the Turkish community had not actually been counted. The same can hardly be said of the published figure of 612,851 for 1976, since the government lacked information on most population movements in the Turkish-controlled zone after July 1974.

After allowing for net migration in the final two inter-censal periods, the true rates of population growth were, approximately:

1931–46	1·82 per cent per annum
1946–60	2·17 per cent per annum

Clearly, a startling change in Cyprus's demographic progress was occurring.

Up to 1931, a feature of Table 1 is the regularity of the pattern – 12 to 15 per cent growth in every decade. To the technician, it suggests that the censuses were of acceptable quality, since such a series of totals, accompanied, as we shall see later, by plausible sex ratios and not unreasonable age distributions, could hardly have resulted from anything other than quite accurate counts of a steadily growing population. For the reader at large, the contrast with earlier growth is noteworthy. Four centuries before the 1881 census counted 186,000 people, the population was about the same, according to the evidence which exists, but then it was to double in some fifty years. Previously it fluctuated rapidly; henceforth, growth would be continuous. Earlier, migration must have been an important factor; in the next fifty years its role was to be only minor. An entirely new pattern of population growth was established around 1881.

That growth in the first fifty years was only moderate – never more than 1½ per cent a year – accorded with the state of the island in general. The first British administrators faced a daunting task. A British consul, Lang, who was an official of the Imperial Ottoman Bank and a farm-owner, wrote of the 'sad record of oppression and misgovernment' under the Turks; Cyprus had been a 'mere estate of the Captain Pasha [governor], and was administered only to produce revenue with no regard to future consequences'. Certainly some improvements had taken place, but no real change in the fundamentally *laissez-faire* attitude of the Turkish government. Even in the last years, rather less than half of the island's revenue was devoted to the island. 'The

Ottoman empire preserved for centuries, as in a museum, the social and political conditions of the Middle Ages', Storrs observed. Modernisation of this small, isolated, impoverished part of an inefficiently governed empire, without notable resources and with only a tiny population, was inevitably drawn out. Some indications of the steps taken by the new government and of the progress made follow.

A nominated Council was appointed to advise the High Commissioner. It was soon replaced by an elected Legislative Council, established under a constitution which proclaimed that the people of the country should take part in the conduct of public affairs. Only the High Commissioner could introduce resolutions for appropriating public revenue and imposing taxes; otherwise members could introduce any subject they pleased. The English, Greek, and Turkish languages might be used orally; bills and minutes would be in English, accompanied by Greek and Turkish translations. Of the twelve elected members, nine were to be Greeks and three Turks, following the proportions found by the 1881 census. Judges were paid adequately for the first time, with new consequences for their impartiality. A target to be attacked immediately was the tax system. The collection of tithes on agricultural produce had been grossly mismanaged. The tax being farmed out by auction, the producer had, in effect, to pay for the farmer's costs and profit in addition to the tax itself – which might or might not be reasonably assessed. 'A tithe of 10 per cent would not have been exorbitant had it been honestly collected . . . other taxes increased the load on the peasant until in an average year he seems to have paid the government from 20 to 25 per cent of his income.'[1] Yet the new rulers retained the tithe – because lack of a land survey and titles to ownership made a land tax impracticable – and it survived until 1926; it was, however, collected directly, not through a farmer. The military exemption tax – in effect a poll tax – was extended to Moslems, who had previously not been liable. If taxation was lightened but little, the peasant gained by being subject to a stable, fairly administered system which encouraged, rather than penalised, expanded cultivation.

The huge backlog of practical work was also tackled, beginning with roads. The Turks' legacy of roads consisted of one, of sorts, from Larnaca to Nicosia, and a few bridges over streams.

According to Consul Lang, every recent Turkish governor had found it his duty to construct a road from Larnaca to Nicosia. Plans were prepared; peasants had to contribute labour or money. Work actually began in 1865, and two years later an estimated £4,000 had been spent, with little result. The project was abandoned – and begun and abandoned again. 'Four times what was required to make the road was extracted from the island, and the road was never made.' After 1878, road building proceeded, by the early 1900s all the main towns were linked, not to speak of Troodos village, at the centre of the main mountain range. A Branch Roads Construction Law was enacted, under which, if a majority of villagers decided in favour of a branch road to link their village to a main road, the government provided half the cost and the able-bodied villagers gave up to six days' work to it. It was a popular measure which was repealed only in 1932. A narrow-guage railway between Famagusta, Nicosia, and Morphou was opened in 1906, and operated until 1950.

Harbours also earned immediate attention, partly for strategic reasons, partly because of the need to expand trade abroad. Most traffic by sea was over open roadsteads at Larnaca and Limassol,[2] Famagusta harbour having been abandoned by the Turks. When the first British troops arrived at Larnaca, a small wooden jetty had hurriedly to be thrown up to receive them. Within three years an iron pier 600 feet long with a depth of water of 20 feet had been constructed at Limassol; a 130-foot jetty at Larnaca followed, together with others at Paphos and Zyyi (for the export of carobs). A mole and quay were constructed at Kyrenia, the only safe harbour on the north coast. Then came the dredging and reconstruction of Famagusta harbour, and by 1904 vessels of 2,000 tons were docking at a quay 900 feet long with 24 feet of water. Yet another aspect of the public communications system was taken in hand. Virtually no postal service existed under the Turks. Now in the six towns the British opened post offices, which were soon dealing in money orders as well as mail. Over a quarter of a million letters were posted in 1884, and by 1905 the Post Office was trying out house-to-house delivery in Nicosia.

Despite progress on these fronts, Cyprus remained far from prosperous for many decades. In 1902, both revenue and expenditure were less than in 1881. Imports and exports had increased only slightly, but in the next thirty years they grew substantially, particularly in the decade which included the Great War; then, it was several years before they exceeded the level reached in 1920. Living standards undoubtedly improved, the government reporting in 1907, for instance, that people's ideas were changing, greater luxuries were being indulged in, whether in Nicosia or the villages, and the air of comfort and prosperity contrasted greatly with the conditions of only a few years previously. 'Poverty as it is in England is unknown.' Ten years later the beneficial effects of the war on the Cypriot economy were noted – merchants made large profits, agricultural products found ready markets with the military in Egypt and Salonika, vine-growers were beginning to free themselves from debt, market gardeners were extending their lands and sinking numerous wells, and villages were improving their housing. Even more important, perhaps, was the psychological effect of the war. As an observer remarked, a new spirit was evident, some eleven thousand Cypriots had joined up as muleteers and in other capacities and had taken their knocks at Salonika and elsewhere, and 'their minds expanded, they saw much in the way of modern methods of farming and mechanics, of busy life in various aspects of which they had never dreamt; and they returned to their country no longer satisfied to rub along in the old ruts'.[3] At the same time the cost of living rose rapidly, and a cheap loaf of equal proportions of wheat and barley flour was produced for the 'urban poor'.

Nevertheless, *The Times* gave a description in 1934 of the pitiful condition of the island – thousands of animals were being killed because they could not feed themselves, people in some districts were on the verge of starvation, the relief work provided by the government was insufficient; and because of indebtedness, the peasant 'had no possible hope of improving his standard of life'.[4] An official document, harking back to the 'unexampled prosperity' of the war years twenty years earlier, saw no hope of a speedy return to the conditions prevailing before the economic depression.[5] Emigration continued – Cypriots were finding employment in places as far afield as the Belgian Congo and elsewhere in Central Africa, while numbers of others went to London, according to the *Annual Report* of 1933. Revenue slumped: in that year, the value of exports was little more than half that of 1929, nor did it regain the same level before the end of the decade. Two years earlier, political unrest had brought about the suspension of the constitution – a situation hardly conducive to international confidence or investment from abroad. Conditions began to change with the coming of war, however. The island suffered no more than a few small and ill-directed air attacks, but in other ways the effects of the war were substantial. Percival termed them 'revolutionary'. The Middle East's involvement in the war 'put the island into a role in world affairs more crucial than it had played since ancient times', and Cyprus became an armed base. Cash was transferred into the economy through the pockets of the allied forces, people of all classes gained unprecedented wealth, and prices, like incomes, rose. Some crops boomed, while others became unsaleable; for the first time, the island ceased to be self-supporting in grain. But, most important of all, jobs became available, and country people, some previously unemployed and many under-employed, commuted to new jobs in the towns and at the army bases, initiating what has been a notable feature of Cypriot life ever since: the daily migration of large numbers of people out of the rural areas. In Meyer's words, the war meant, among other things, 'relief from the drab monotony of life in the island's villages'. Thousands of Cypriots joined the forces and many served abroad. Consequently, a significant proportion of the younger male population – not to speak of a few women, who also served with distinction – eventually returned home, not only with ready cash to their names, but, more important, with new ideas from the world overseas. The government, having increased revenues, could plan for the future on a basis of greater activity and responsibility than ever before, the *Annual Report* observed. The 1946 ten-year development programme was costed at £5·8 millions, but it was foreseen that £6.3 millions could actually be found. Annual revenue was running at £3 millions, and the national debt amounted to less than half that sum. 'Cyprus is in an exceptionally strong position in respect of its borrowings', the development programme noted.

Following on the war, the economy continued to flourish, and the standard of living to rise. International events, culminating in the withdrawal from Suez, led Britain to continue using the island as a base. The mining industry came into its own, as the price of copper soared and the value of Cyprus's cupreous and iron pyrites rose proportionately; when the peak was reached in 1956, mineral exports paid for about a quarter of the ordinary governmental operating expenses. The Korean war and the resulting shortages of goods and shipping space served to benefit local industry. Emigrants' remittances, amounting to perhaps £8 a year per head of population, helped to feed the economy. In the 1950s, Britain expanded her bases considerably, so more jobs than ever were available, and local service and manufacturing industries grew apace. The national income per capita doubled in some eight years, so that even after allowing for considerable inflation, its increase was consistently high by any standards.

The boom lasted until 1957, when several reasons brought about a downward trend. The price of copper fell to half the level of a few years earlier, and in addition, the island's high-grade ore was becoming exhausted; consequently, revenue fell, and so did public spending. The expansion of the bases had to come to an end, and it was in 1957, when the work was nearing completion, that expenditure was cut by 20 per cent. The civil disturbances which broke out in 1955 discouraged economic activity and halted the growing tourist industry. By chance, some general recession coincided with local weather conditions which were unfavourable to agriculture. The balance of trade was unhealthy, as imports came to be worth nearly double the country's exports, and while invisible earnings, notably British forces' spending and emigrants' remittances, bridged the gap for the time, their future levels could only be uncertain. Both national income and investment fell in the final years of the 1950s. Emigration, on the other hand, increased, and a good deal of private capital reportedly left the island. In 1960, a United Nations mission observed '. . . the Cyprus economy . . . seemed to be running along a downhill and rather bumpy road'. From that point, the economic situation became more closely linked with political events which are outside the scope of this study, so it suffices to note that the uncertainty of 1960 was not confirmed subsequently; on the contrary, the economy was recovering well until interrupted by inter-communal disagreement, sporadic fighting, and the progressive separation of the two main communities. By 1967, an economist was able to write 'there seems little doubt that the Greek sector of the island has fully recovered and, indeed, is again enjoying a boom period' – and also to note that 'since

1963 the Turkish sector has failed to share in the rising prosperity of the rest of the island. Turkish unemployment is high, and average incomes have fallen by one half'.[6] That contrast continues today, as marked as ever. In the area controlled by the government, the term 'economic miracle' is heard, and despite great loss of resources and displacement of population in 1974, exports exceed pre-1974 levels, unemployment hardly exists except in certain professional occupations, agriculture has undergone further change for the better, the construction and tourist industries flourish, capital is available for investment, emigration may almost have ceased. The Turkish-Cypriot authorities claim, on the other hand, that before 1974 their community had a mere 5 per cent of the island's gross domestic product and an economy with the characteristics of an undeveloped agricultural community,[7] so it is not surprising that in 1979 an observer could report that 80 per cent of the north's export revenue came from agriculture, and production of the most important item, citrus fruits, had yet to regain the pre-1974 level; that industry remained little developed; and that there was great discontent at the economic situation.[8] In 1979, the cost of living rose by 75 per cent, according to official sources.[9] It is difficult to foresee marked improvement for the Turkish-Cypriots in the future, as they continue to be unrecognised internationally and therefore to encounter barriers in trade and communications, and to be linked economically to a motherland which itself has exceptional problems.

Agriculture has always been a vital sector of the economy, but on the whole it received less than its fair share of attention in the early British years, partly because of the urgent need for public works, partly because of farmers' conservatism. Yet perhaps the most wide-reaching advance was made in this field – the virtual elimination of the locust. Drought and locusts had always been farming's greatest hazards, turning it into a big gamble which the peasants faced with a fatalistic outlook, as one historian remarked. The Turks made sporadic attempts at controlling the pest; in 1867, for instance, every peasant was obliged to bring in some eighty pounds of locusts' eggs, which were then destroyed. They were unsuccessful, for in 1881 the High Commissioner could write of the locusts' depredations: 'With marvellous rapidity and utterly regardless of any interruption, they strip off every green thing, and in a few hours the green patches they attack disappear, leaving a few brown sticks issuing from what appears to be a fallow field.' The system of control used after 1878 and invented twenty years earlier by an Italian landowner in Cyprus, Richard Mattei, was based on the observation that locusts, once on the march, do not turn back. So traps were laid across the line of march – canvas cloths set at an acute angle to the ground and topped with oil cloth; unable to pass over them, the locusts fell back into specially dug pits which, when full, were closed with earth. The scale of the operation was enormous. In 1884 it was reported that the screens in use would have stretched for 315 miles, almost long enough to encircle the entire coastline; one single screen actually extended for twenty-seven miles; and some 56 billion locusts had been destroyed – less than a third of the number in the previous year! Over 1,300 labourers were employed. They and their equipment were financed by a special tax, but if the action taken turned out to be successful, it would be more than recouped to the people in a single year, the High Commissioner observed. After 1887 virtually no damage was caused by locusts; and in 1901, the *Annual Report* was able to state that the scourge had ended. With the locusts, the risk of famine also largely disappeared.

Other aspects of agriculture were not neglected either, but investigating the problems needed time; for example, Consul Lang, who introduced English ploughs, 'was not long in finding out that much that was good in the West was unsuitable to the East', and so turned to searching for the best quality of locally used implements, bullocks and seed. The results he obtained from them surpassed expectations. Following on a visit by the Director of the Imperial Institute of London in 1904, an Agriculture Department was set up and charged with conducting agricultural experiments and studying local methods with a view to improving them in the light of modern knowledge – Lang's course of thirty-five years earlier. An agricultural college was founded; nursery gardens were opened; a pest which attacked the carob tree and vine blight were investigated and combated; thoroughbred stallions and Devon bulls and milch cows were imported for the government's stock farm; travelling supervisors advised villagers on agricultural matters. Long-term hopes must have been high, since earlier observers had been able to make

42

comments such as 'within a single farm lie zones of culture for which we might elsewhere have to go half round the world'. In the 1930s they seemed nearer fulfilment, as prices improved with the Italo-Abyssinian war, and exports of wine and potatoes increased. During the European war, effort was concentrated in maximising food production, and farmers profited from the increased demand arising from the presence of allied forces; yet in 1946 Percival could still observe that agriculture 'provides the farmer with a very poor standard of living'. Twenty-five years later, when agriculture employed under 40 per cent of all workers, farming provided a far better return. What brought about the change? It is relevant to recall another remark of Percival's – that the Cyprus farmer had, in the face of great climatic and political handicaps, achieved a lot in establishing a remarkable range of products, including many of fine quality; he possessed both toughness and skill.

Seasonal crop failures due to drought were the chief reason for the money-lending which shackled agriculture, most farmers lacking the capital to finance one bad season, let alone the two or three which could occur. Virtually uncontrolled by the government, the system worked as described in 1889: 'Interest to be at 24 per cent; the payment to be made in kind, even if the ingathering of the produce is approaching; a juggling theft at the time the produce is weighed; and moreover when the entries are made in the book, if the produce that is given to the peasant on credit is barley which is worth 1 piastre the kilo, it is put down at 3 piastres; if rice worth 3d the oke, at 9d, and so forth in the same proportion, the capital also being charged with interest.' If the season was good, the loan was recovered at harvest time; if not, the debt was renewed, and after one or two repetitions, many farmers were left without means to repay. The island's prisons overflowed with debtors, it was reported, and their number was reduced only when the government required creditors to contribute to their debtors' maintenance. Despite the existence of a Public Loan Fund from 1897, a Commission to Enquire into the Extent, Cause and Effect of Indebtedness in the Island reported in 1918 that some money-lenders charged interest at three or four shillings in the pound, despite the legal maximum of, first, 9 per cent and, later, 12 per cent, and further, as bonds were renewed every few months, interest became compounded. 'The mass of long-term debt owed to money-lenders constitutes the most serious burden on the country' was the opinion in 1935 of Oakden, who pointed out that since the loans often included no provision for repayment, the usurer looked on them as an investment and the client remained as heavily indebted as ever after years of work; consequently, it was only natural that peasants lacked interest in improving productivity. Remedying this situation would clearly take time, but the essential step was taken in 1940, when a Debt Settlement Board was established, to which both debtors and creditors might submit claims. In the Board's five years, about 14,000 farmers made application to it – a third, perhaps, of their total number. Debts were reduced by some 35 per cent on average, and fair repayment terms were established. Nevertheless, farmers still needed credit, since many could not finance their operations for a year in advance, let alone survive a season's drought, and it was then that cooperative societies came into their own. A Cooperative Societies Law had existed since 1914, and the Agricultural Bank, formed in 1925, used the societies as its agents. Small though the Bank's start was, it prompted a member of the Legislative Council – himself a merchant, we may assume – to observe: 'I regret to say that the Agricultural Bank has done a lot of good in my district.'[10] A Cooperative Department was created in 1935, and a Cooperative Central Bank in 1937. Thus, an organisation capable of replacing the money-lender in rural life was in existence, and it did so, taking over his multiple functions of banking, marketing, and supplying consumer needs. Cooperatives expanded subsequently, until by the 1970s they possibly had a greater role in the economy and life of Cyprus than in any other country.

The intricate sub-division of land was another reason for slow agricultural development. Land was transmissible by inheritance within certain degrees of relationship, but not by will, and custom or law maintained the principle of equal inheritance of parental immovable property by all offspring; consequently, fragmentation increased in geometrical progression. Further, trees, buildings, and the water supply could be owned separately from the land on which they stood. Extreme cases were reported of a carob tree owned by over a hundred co-heirs, and of a well divided into nearly three million shares which were owned in differing proportions by nine different people, and the 1946 census report observed: 'For the farmer of 70 donums [about 25 acres] with 13 parcels of land uniformly spaced, it may be calculated that to visit each parcel he would have to cover 22.8 miles. Although this figure is a purely arithmetical conception, it nevertheless gives a reasonable picture of the layout of Cyprus farms.' In 1969, the government initiated long-term measures to rectify this extreme fragmentation. By then, the average farm holding had shrunk to something like fifteen acres, and a survey of the Limassol plain showed that fragmentation ranged from one plot to 142 plots per ownership, with an average of 3.3 plots and an average plot size of under two acres. The first step was to enact a Land Consolidation Law, with the object of redistributing land so that farmers came to own compact holdings of about the same value as the land they held originally. Consolidation could be effected by various means - agreement among a number of owners, a majority resolution among the farmers concerned, or, very exceptionally, a government order. By 1974, the first four operations, each of about village size, were successfully completed, and subsequently one or two more in the government-controlled area have followed in each year. While not everyone has been satisfied with the results, the Ministry of Agriculture reckons on a level of agreement among the farmers concerned of 70 per cent – aided by incentives such as the right to a country road, built at the expense of the Land Fund, to each plot. Some problems remain to be solved in continuing this lengthy process in the future – for example how to deal with land owned by Turkish-Cypriots and with water rights when their ownership is not identical with that of the land.

The supreme agricultural problem, shortage of water, was reviewed by a geologist as early as 1881, but with few short-term results: reservoirs constructed on the Mesaoria plain ran dry just when water was needed. Irrigation was not a new idea: the medieval plantations of sugar cane and cotton had been irrigated, and towards the end of the Turkish era there was some private development of water wheels and chains-of-wells. The latter were underground conduits, set at an inclination less than that of the surface, so that the water eventually arrived above ground. They derived their name from the shafts for ventiliation or the disposal of earth which were dug at intervals, giving the appearance of a series of wells. Although more chains-of-wells were built, systematic exploitation of the scarce water resources had to wait for many years. However, when the Agriculture Department's report for 1959 stated that the most important change in land use in the past ten years had been the development of irrigated crops for export – citrus, potatoes, and other vegetables – it referred to the most exciting development in Cyprus's agriculture ever to have taken place. Its significance is emphasised by the statistic that at about that time, citrus fruit occupied some 1 per cent of the agricultural land, produced 10 per cent of the gross agricultural income, and was responsible for almost a third of agricultural exports by value. Even so, the crop's requirements of perennial irrigation had kept its cultivation within tiny limits.

Little progress with irrigation had been achieved before 1945. Two reservoirs were constructed in the 1930s, but were unsuccessful; then circumstances became unfavourable for capital investment. But by 1945 motives such as the high price of potatoes for export and the growing market abroad for citrus fruits prompted farmers to seek more and more water for irrigation. In 1946, 8,000 acres were irrigated for the first time. Two dams were built, weirs were constructed, attention was given to canals, tanks and masonry channels, a big chain-of-wells in the south-east corner of the island was nearing completion – the largest perennial irrigation project yet undertaken – and eighty-three boreholes were drilled with the aid of government subsidies. With the help of contributions from the beneficiaries, work was concentrated in the 1950s on many small schemes rather than a few big ones – gravity irrigation from springs and rivers, storage in artificial reservoirs, the pumping of irrigation water. In 1952, for instance, 125 schemes were completed, irrigating some 4,000 acres, 185 boreholes were drilled for irrigation, and total irrigated land had increased by 24 per cent since 1946. By 1955, proposals for such schemes were fewer, and the cost and difficulty of irrigating each additional acre was increasing, the Irrigation Department observed, but all the same, 135 boreholes were drilled in that year, and 14 per cent of all arable land was now irrigated in an average winter and 5 per cent in an average summer. Such development brought problems: near Famagusta, pumping had lowered the water table to twenty feet below sea level, and many citrus groves were ruined owing to the penetration of sea water. In 1964, ten dams were completed or were under construction, river training, draining, and recharge schemes were carried out, together with seventy-two minor irrigation schemes, and since 1946, 1,315 successful irrigation boreholes (i.e. giving over 1,000 gallons an hour) had been drilled, and the area of perennially irrigated land had trebled. Shortly after, a comprehensive national water plan was being prepared, and in the twenty years following 1960, storage capacity rose from 6 to 106 million cubic metres. A splendid example of this work can easily be seen today at Yermasoyia, where a dam 140 feet high (over its lowest foundation) has created a lake which helps irrigate the Akrotiri peninsula and a beauty spot which delights the people of Limassol every summer week-end. Today, the biggest project ever undertaken on the island is under way in the government-controlled area, designed to irrigate some 13,000 acres along the Paphos coast, and an even bigger scheme, enigmatically named the Southern Conveyor, will link all the significant water sources in the southern part of the island with the main demand centres.

The change in the land use pattern reported by the Agriculture Department in 1959, of fundamental importance to the island, may be illustrated by a few figures. The production of cereals did not vary very greatly between 1900 and 1974, but that of potatoes, other vegetables, and citrus fruits rose sharply and continuously after 1945; for instance, exports of potatoes were worth C£953,000 in 1952, C£2 million in 1963 and C£7 million in 1972. Production of citrus fruit increased five-fold between 1936 and 1956, when exports were worth C£1,650,000, and by 1972 the corresponding figure was over C£12 million. In the mid-1960s, produce from the one-tenth of cropped land which was irrigated accounted for around 50 per cent of the value of agricultural output and for about three-quarters of agricultural exports. Turning to a different measure, the author was told in Paphos that irrigation increases the value of a farmer's output there up by to seven times – a simplification, no doubt, which possibly fails to allow for increased water charges and other novel expenses, but nevertheless a clear explanation of the drive to change the pattern of agriculture.

Mechanisation has been another important factor in agricultural progress. Because landholdings were small and scattered, individual ownership of farm machinery was often impracticable, but this proved little obstacle to its increasing use, which was organised by cooperatives or contractors. Twenty-seven tractors were in use in 1939; the number had increased to 319 by 1948 even though machines were in short supply; it then rose to 4,000 in 1963, when 360 combine harvesters were also operating, together with a variety of other equipment such as rotary hoes, grain drills, fertiliser spreaders, and potato planters. Growing official support for agriculture included the following measures. A Crop Provident Fund was introduced in 1956, and its successor, the Agricultural Provident Fund Scheme, paid out over C£5 million in 1963 alone for crop losses caused by drought. The Agriculture Department, later the Department of Agriculture of the Ministry of Agriculture and Natural Resources, increased its activity in research, practical assistance and training, for instance in soil surveying and analysis, setting up livestock and dairy units, and maintaining high standards of exported produce by means of inspection. A quasi-governmental Grain Commission regulated the import of all grains, and purchased local cereals at a fixed price; it was thus in a position to provide encouragement for new planting, and in most years the price paid did, in fact, include an element of subsidy.

Once the pride of the island, its forests had suffered such depredations that even the Turks were obliged to restrict felling. With evidence in 1880 that for every hundred trees standing, seventy-two others had been felled and their timber was lying on the ground to rot, while for every hundred standing there were only twenty-five seedlings, the total disappearance of the forest was only a matter of time. Within a year the British restricted felling, and a commission was set up to delimit all forest areas as a preliminary to controlling felling and grazing. Such stern measures led to a temporary need to import firewood, but, as the Forestry Adviser observed, without them 'the Mediterranean would soon count one island less and one rock more'. Grazing by goats – a subject on which feelings ran high – was controlled too, the first step being to license the presence of goats in selected forest blocks on a rotating basis, thus giving others the time to regenerate. The problem was intractable, and was still being considered by official committees fifty years later. Nursery gardens were established, one as early as 1878. Eucalyptus and acacias were grown as well as the native pines and cypress, and were soon distributed over the island, the eucalyptus serving to hold down sand dunes, protect the banks of streams from erosion, redeem marshland, and as firewood. Despite slow initial progress, by the 1930s advantages were accruing from a vigorous forest policy – the checking of the run-off of the winter rains and of erosion, and the consequent conservation of the water supply.

Manufacturing existed on only a very small scale before the Second World War, being limited to producing minor amounts of goods such as cotton and silk materials, leather, tiles and bricks, pottery, jam, and cheese. As the High Commissioner observed in 1891, manufactures were few in number and inconsiderable in extent, whereas in the Middle Ages they were numerous and had a great reputation. Mining of copper had had a long history which went back at least as far as Roman times. The mines were closed for a very long period including the Lusignan, Venetian, and Turkish regimes, but, reopening on a large scale after the First World War, soon had two thousand employees. Asbestos, gypsum, and umber were worked in modest quantities, and the supply of asbestos-bearing rock was thought to be inexhaustible. Then, as will be seen in Chapter 7, a move away from agricultural occupations began in the 1940s. What were the industries which led people to leave agriculture? The construction work which boomed during the war and in the 1950s continued to flourish subsequently, as new housing, office accommodation and hotels appeared in every town and modern houses began to replace village cottages, and in 1973 the building industry occupied about 10 per cent of the labour force. Indeed, almost every sector of the economy except agriculture increased in importance up to 1974, including manufacturing, which in that year gave work to some 14 per cent of all workers, even though it still accounted for less than 5 per cent of exports by value. Manufacturing had continued to be small scale, and by 1960 only the production of wine was substantial, but then an effort to utilise local raw materials was made, and the canning industry resulted, using local fruits and fruit juices. The next step was to manufacture substitutes for imported goods such as washing powders, textiles, footwear, and furniture, and here notable progress was made in the years after 1965, as the Middle East became rich and Cyprus' manufacturers and exporters were quick to respond to the opportunity. By 1978, almost 18 per cent of all workers in the

49

government-controlled area worked in manufacturing, and even so, labour shortages were beginning to appear, a few foreigners were actually imported for factory work, and managers were directing future strategy towards increased automation. This was a remarkable development within four years of the south being so flooded with refugees that it had an acknowledged unemployment rate of 30 per cent and a real one of much more; the term 'miracle' used by an industrialist to the author in discussing his own surprising labour shortage hardly seems exaggerated.

The ethnic groups

Great changes in the economy and standards of living occurred, then, after 1940, but far from equally in the two major communities after 1963. Did their demographic progress also differ, both before and after those dates? The growth of both groups is shown in Table 2.

In Cyprus' statistics the dividing line between race and religion has been blurred, but in practice little confusion has existed. Generally, 'Greek' has been synonymous in Cyprus with 'Christian', and 'Moslem' with 'Turkish'. The earlier censuses included a question about the individual's religion, but not his race. Not until 1960 was a question on race asked – in addition to one on religion; and then the differentiation seemed uncertain, as both classifications included 'Maronite'. The Maronites are a Christian sect in Lebanon, of which a number moved to Cyprus long ago, and their very name derives from a fifth-century saint, Maron; yet they were considered a race, as well as a religion, by the 1960 census. No further data on religions have been collected subsequently, but a different complication has appeared recently with 'Turkish-Cypriots', a term not found previously in the lists of either religions or races. Writing of the Turkish era, Papadopoullos states that, for Islam, religious assimilation meant a concurrent change of ethnic status, inasmuch as religious and political status were two inextricable qualities in Islamic law; a Christian embracing Islam was considered an Ottoman from that moment. Percival made the same point in a different way: religion and mother tongue, he asserted, were the clearest and most easily identified attributes of what were in fact racial and political communities. And on the foundation of the Republic in 1960, the

TABLE 2: THE GROWTH OF THE GREEK ORTHODOX AND
MOSLEM COMMUNITIES, 1881–1978

Census of	Number Greek Orthodox	Moslem	Annual increase per cent Greek Orthodox	Moslem
1881	137,631	45,458		
1891	158,585	47,926	1·42	0·53
1901	182,739	51,309	1·42	0·69
1911	214,480	56,428	1·62	0·93
1921	244,887	61,339	1·33	0.84
1931	276,572	64,238	1·23	0·46
1946	361,199	80,548	1·80	1·52
1960	442,363	104,333	1·46	1·87
1973	482,000 (approx.)		0·69	
1976	480—488,000 (approx.)			
(1978		145,000		1·85)

Note: In 1973 and 1976, the classification was of race, not religion, and the
enumeration was conducted *de jure*. Earlier, the classification was of
religion, and the enumerations were *de facto*. The Turkish-Cypriot total
of 1978 is *de facto*. (*De facto* signifies presence on census day. *De jure*
signifies normally resident, i.e. excluding temporary visitors but including
residents temporarily absent.)

new Constitution – according to which the public service, armed
forces, and police were to comprise specified proportions of
Greeks and Turks – formalised the coincidence of race and
religion in the following definitions: 'The Greek community
comprises all citizens of the Republic who are of Greek origin and
whose mother tongue is Greek or who share the Greek cultural
traditions or who are members of the Greek Orthodox Church.'
The point was made even more clearly in the next paragraph of
Article 2, which defined the Turkish community in a similar way,
using the terms 'Turkish origin', 'whose mother tongue is
Turkish', the 'Turkish cultural tradition' and 'who are *Moslems*'.
Most censuses made a further, and related, enquiry – on
mother tongue. Every time it was found that the numbers of
Greek-speakers and of the Greek Orthodox were not quite the

same; and similarly with persons having Turkish as their mother tongue and Moslems. In 1931, for example, nearly 3 per cent of the Moslems spoke Greek as their mother tongue. In 1881 that proportion had been over 5 per cent. These figures remind us that some Greek-speakers were converted to Islam in the Turkish era; Percival, for his part, made a different point – that the Turks in certain areas had become so closely bound to the surrounding Greek population as to have abandoned the Turkish language. Perhaps both theories help to explain the differentials found by the censuses.

Some amplification of Table 2 is needed.

(a) The 1960 report tabulated both religion and race, the latter figure being the higher by 0·2 per cent. In 1973 and 1976, the numerical differences between race and religion must again have been small, so the difference in classifications in this table may be disregarded for practical purposes.

(b) Since the 1973 census did not give a *de facto* total, there is no indication of the adjustment necessary to compare the *de facto* total of 1960 with the *de jure* figure in 1973. Almost certainly a *de jure* count of Greek-Cypriots exceeds one conducted *de facto*. The adjustment required could have been considerable, since over 12,000 Cypriots, excluding Turkish-Cypriots, were reported to be studying abroad in 1976 and the detail of year of study suggests that the total three years earlier was little less. Further, some Cypriot tourists are usually abroad at any given time. If 10,000 of the 1973 *de jure* population were absent from Cyprus during the enumeration, the increase since 1960 would have been 6·7, not 9·0 per cent, and the annual rate of increase 0·52 instead of 0·69 per cent.

(c) The 1973 and 1976 totals omit the Armenian and Maronite communities, since neither was included in the Greek Orthodox totals up to 1960.

(d) In 1976 some 8,000 persons working abroad may have been incorrectly omitted from the *de jure* count. The true total should, then, be within the range shown.

(e) The reliability of the 1978 figure for Turkish-Cypriots is unknown, in the absence of information on how it was obtained.

The Turkish-Cypriot authorities have stated that a *de facto* census was taken in January 1975, but because a substantial part of the Turkish-Cypriot population was then outside the area under Turkish-Cypriot control, 'the census in question was not deemed to be complete and valid. Nevertheless the results obtained have formed the basis for calculating the population estimates of 1978.'[11] We may suspect a lack of both expertise and organisation at the time, but also think that counting the small Turkish-Cypriot population with the aid of 1,500 enumerators[12] was a comparatively easy task. Uncertainty regarding some other components in the 1978 total also exists: it is not known whether net migration between January 1975 and 1978 is fully accounted for, or natural increase either, in the absence of complete registration of births and deaths. However, the published total seems worth recording, with some reservation about its accuracy.

As the Greek population increased annually by 1·62 per cent early in the century, a rate of 1·80 per cent from 1931 to 1946 was not outstanding. But because the rate had decreased after 1911, it seems surprising to find an upsurge of as much as 50 per cent occurring twenty to thirty years later. The contributions to this unusual pattern of changing fertility, mortality and migration will be examined subsequently. After 1946, a different type of change is evident. Between that date and 1960 emigration grew and could have been a significant factor in the falling rate, but since an initially modest reduction later turned into a spectacular decline, it is fair to suppose that a good part of the fall after 1946 was due to natural causes. By the 1960s the Greek population was growing more slowly than at any time since records were kept, and the pace of the decline suggested that eventual reversion to earlier norms was unlikely. Later, the 1973 census results confirmed statistically what was already obvious to the observer – that for many people, certainly the town-dwellers, there was a firm trend towards smaller families. It is not known whether growth declined further by 1976, partly because some inaccuracy in the count of that year would not be surprising, partly because of uncertainty about demographic events around 1974 – emigration was not fully recorded, how many emigrants later returned to Cyprus is not known and official figures of casualties have not been issued. With a recorded decrease in those years, there are certainly no grounds to suppose that natural increase was growing again.

Before 1931, the Moslem community increased in a quite different fashion. Except for the emigration of some five thousand in the mid-1920s, there is no obvious explanation for the far slower growth – 41 per cent in fifty years, against 101 per cent for the Greeks. The differential was observed very early, the High Commissioner writing of the 1891 census: 'What is more noticeable is the fact of the actual increase of the Mahomedan population, that being, it is said, against the experience of the neighbouring Mahomedan countries of the Turkish empire.' Possibly it was indicative of comparative standards of living that while Greek growth of 15 per cent in a decade passed without comment, any increase at all of the Turkish-Cypriots caused surprise. Thirty years later, another High Commissioner recorded his explanation: 'There has been a tendency for the Mohamedan population to decrease, due principally to a gradual return to Turkey and to the poverty of the Turkish villager in comparison with his Greek compatriot.'

Obviously emigration was a possible reason for slower Turkish-Cypriot growth. Did others exist, for instance lower fertility? Unfortunately no information on family size in the two communities became available. But the census of 1946 was to discover that births per female averaged *more* among Turkish-Cypriots than Greek-Cypriots, and as all ages were included, some women then enumerated were having their children well before 1931. Of mortality, no evidence either way has been discovered.

Although it would have been natural for some Turks to leave after their occupation ended, no sizeable exodus was noted, and perhaps the number who went was small, for the Turkish-Cypriot peasant, like his Greek neighbour, had been hard pressed by the old regime, and probably – and correctly – foresaw little harm to either his livelihood or his religion in the change. But Lang had noticed just *before* 1878 that the Christians were increasing more rapidly than the Moslems – owing, he thought, to the conscription which fell on the Moslems but not on the Greeks; some emigration of the former was implied. More Turks left later, probably, as the Greeks not only assumed leading positions everywhere, but voiced their desire for union with

Greece in no uncertain terms. For instance, in their memorandum of 1907, on the visit of Mr Churchill, Under-Secretary of State for the Colonies, they confidently expected the realisation of their desire – union with Greece, adding that the small Mohammedan minority might disapprove of the fulfilment of that historical national right of the Cypriot Hellenes, but that its numbers were not strong enough to entitle it to dispose of the national fate; nor could it be alleged that its real activity in civilising and in economic progress was possessed of any significance – every work connected with mental or economic progress was almost exclusively exercised by the Cypriot Hellenes. For many decades, independence for Cyprus was hardly in prospect, so the Turkish community had no reason to fear a shared, but predominantly Greek, government, but they did have grounds to foresee rule by Greece, in which they were unlikely to have much say. In emigrating, patriotic feeling for the Turkish motherland seems not to have been important; there is no record that Turkish-Cypriots went there in 1914 on the entry of Turkey into the war as Britain's enemy, and when British nationality was later conferred on Ottoman subjects resident on the island unless they stated a preference for Ottoman citizenship and were prepared to leave the island within a specified time, not one applied to remain Ottoman. Economic reasons were certainly the more significant factor. Unfortunately the emigration they motivated was not always successful, particularly around 1921, when the *Annual Report* recorded that large numbers of Cypriots who had recently sought work abroad were destitute and had to be repatriated. Nevertheless, some 8 per cent of the Turks, including people of education, social standing and enterprise, took the opportunity of moving to Turkey following on the Treaty of Lausanne in 1923. There had been some highly selective emigration too, Percival discovered: 'A search of the records shows that in the past it was for a time the custom for Moslems from the mainland to come to Cyprus in search of brides, to an extent which aroused much anxiety in the local Moslem community.'[13]

It must have been relevant that with Turkey only forty miles away, movement to and fro was easy – far easier than for Greek-Cypriots to move to Egypt or Greece. Emigration to Greece was, in fact, seldom mentioned in contemporary records, and perhaps small outflows to both Greece and Turkey went unnoticed amid the more momentous migrations to Egypt, the USA, Central Africa, and even Australia. In the village, leaving for America must have been a stirring event, since the migrant would probably never return; taking a small boat to Mersin, on the other hand, was probably easier than going from Paphos to Nicosia. Culturally, too, ties with Turkey may have been closer than with Greece, if only because no sizeable immigration from Greece had occurred since ancient times, whereas the Turkish community was little more than three hundred years old. It remains to add that the views sought by the author of many individuals for the differential in growth of the two communities up to 1931 – and indeed 1946 – have almost all leaned to emigration of Turkish-Cypriots. No one consulted thought Turkish fertility to have been lower than that of the Greeks; concerning mortality, no views were obtained. On balance, emigration was probably the main reason for that interesting feature of Cypriot demographic history, the lower growth rate of the Turkish community between 1881 and 1946; slightly higher mortality accompanying a lower level of prosperity may also have been a factor.

Had some 5,000 Turkish-Cypriots not emigrated to Turkey in the mid-1920s, the community would have totalled about 70,000 in 1931. The increase of 14 per cent in the decade would then have exceeded the Greek-Cypriot increase, but as some Greek-Cypriots emigrated too, the *natural* increase of the two communities was probably similar, according well with the small differential found in 1931–46, leading to *higher* Turkish-Cypriot growth in 1946–60. Taking the point a stage further: if the Turkish-Cypriot community had, like the Greek-Cypriots, increased by 101 per cent between 1881 and 1931, it would have totalled 91,300 in 1931 – 27,000 more than the number enumerated. Is it possible that so many Turkish-Cypriots emigrated in the fifty-year period? Taken together, the considerations just mentioned suggest that it probably was. From a base of 45,000 in 1881, emigration of anything like 27,000 persons seems huge, but after subtracting the known 5,000 of the 1920s, the balance represents an average annual outflow of some 500 – not enough, probably, to concern the community's leaders, evoke official comment, or be documented in any way which survives today.

A startling change occurred in the Turkish-Cypriots' growth

rate after 1931: it more than trebled, from 0·46 per cent a year in the previous decade to 1·52 per cent a year up to 1946. However, we surmised earlier that *natural* growth between 1921 and 1931 was about 1·31 per cent annually, and that being the case, the increase to 1·52 per cent was not surprising. Indeed, it fits neatly into a series rising to 1·87 per cent between 1946 and 1960, and forms a pattern far from inconsonant with the improving economic conditions of the time. It remains, then, to question whether Turkish-Cypriot natural increase could really have continued to grow after 1946 while that of the Greeks fell, or whether the two quite different growth patterns of that time – illustrated in Figure 1 – resulted from migration rather than natural causes. Clearly there have always been cultural differences between the two communities, and it is generally thought that an economic differential existed too, the advantage lying on the Greek side. Experience suggests that differing demographic trends can be due in part to such factors; and it is certain that the 'demographic transition', the change from a state of high fertility and high mortality to low fertility and low mortality, occurs at varying times in different communities. Consequently there is no essential reason why Greek-Cypriot and Turkish-Cypriot fertility should have reached their peak at the same time. Further, it was in 1946 that the census indicated higher fertility among the latter – a point of obvious importance to the growth of the communities in the next fourteen years. We may conclude, therefore, that higher natural growth among the Turkish-Cypriots after 1946 was perfectly feasible.

Can the accuracy of their 1978 estimate be assessed? It implies an annual rate of increase since 1960 of 1·85 per cent. Since that rate is very slightly lower than the previous inter-censal rate, it is obviously not impossible. Further, it is considerably below the annual increases estimated for nearby Moslem countries at about the same time – 2·4 per cent in Turkey, 3·3 in Syria, 2·2 in Egypt. Had the Turkish-Cypriot population increased after 1960 at the rate estimated for Turkey in the first half of the 1970s, it would have numbered 160,000 in 1978, not 145,000. Further, data from two sources other than the Statistics Department may be compared with that Department's tabulation of age in single years in 1978.[14] First, an enummeration conducted in March 1980 by the Elections Commission resulted in a preliminary total

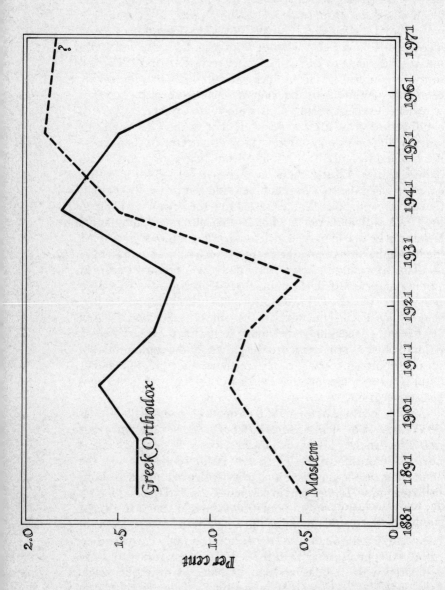

Figure 1. Annual rates of increase of the Greek-Orthodox and Moslem communities

of 80,500 persons entitled to vote, that is with local nationality and aged 18 and over. According to the Department of Statistics' tabulation, 91,038 persons were 18 and over in 1978. Once allowance is made for the inexperienced methodology of both counts, for particularly difficult circumstances at the time of the 1975 enumeration, for uncertainty on the part of some respondents around 18 about their exact age, for migration since 1978, and for the presence in 1980 of some foreigners not entitled to vote,[15] the comparison is not unreasonable. Another listing was made by the Commission in March 1981, resulting provisionally in 83,800 voters plus 6,200 non-voters aged 18 and over – figures which are still closer to the Department of Statistics' estimates. Secondly, 18,328 children reportedly attended primary school in 1977–78, while children aged 7 to 12, that is to say of primary school age, totalled 18,526. In the following year, when junior secondary schooling became compulsory, the number attending at that level was reported to be 11,200, while children aged 13 to 15 totalled 10,701 according to the population data. That children enter and leave school in accordance with school terms, not their birthdays, can easily account for the small discrepancies seen here. Cross-checks of data issued by different branches of the Turkish-Cypriot authority therefore do nothing to contradict the 1978 population estimate. In summary, the total of 145,000 was not only perfectly feasible on demographic grounds but could have been higher – much higher if some immigration is assumed; no information has been made available to the author which suggests any marked inaccuracy in that total; but as experience shows that enumerations made in difficult circumstances are not always accurate, minor weaknesses in the 1975 count and, therefore, in the 1978 data would not be surprising.

Differing rates of growth in the two communities naturally led to changes in the composition of the population, as shown in Table 3. The large proportion of 'Other religions' in 1960 was due to the inclusion in the census of more British servicemen and families than previously. Were they excluded, it would be found that the proportion of the Greek Orthodox decreased by only half a per cent in 1960, while that of the Moslems increased correspondingly.

The consistently decreasing proportion of Moslems up to 1946 is noteworthy. As for the 'other religions', they comprised

TABLE 3: THE COMPOSITION OF THE POPULATION BY
RELIGION, 1881–1960 (PERCENTAGES)

Census of	Greek Orthodox	Moslem	Other religions*
1881	73·9	24·4	1·7
1901	77·1	21·6	1·3
1921	78·8	19·7	1·5
1931	79·5	18·5	2·0
1946	80·2	17·9	1·9
1960	77·0	18·3	4·7

* Includes Armenians and Maronites

Maronites, Armenians, Roman Catholics, and Jews. All were
long-established in Cyprus. The numbers of Jews enumerated
were negligible, but their history was the oldest, for some were
resident in Cyprus before the Christian era; they were wiped out
in the second century AD, after which no sizeable Jewish
community ever inhabited Cyprus again. The Maronites moved
into Cyprus during or before the Lusignan period, numbering
7–8,000 and occupying thirty villages. They still held four
villages in the 1850s, but by 1931 numbered no more than 1,700.
The reason for the decline was not re-emigration, but rather
absorption into the Greek community. At the same date,
Armenians numbered 3,300, most of whom had immigrated as a
result of the First World War. There had, however, been
Armenians in the island's army which resisted King Richard of
England in 1191, Armenian villages existed under the Lusignans,
and their presence was noted by a traveller in 1738, who added
that they were poor. Today they are town-dwellers, many of them
in business or the civil service and, unlike the Maronites, are little
interested in agriculture. The number of Roman Catholics was
only 1,014 in 1931; a few were foreigners, but most were,
perhaps, descendants of the earlier Franks and Venetians. All
these religious groups are treated with perfect tolerance, and two
at least, the Maronites and the Armenians, have a standing in the
life of the country out of proportion to their numbers.

Little comparison of Turkish increase in Cyprus and Turkey is
possible, for lack of data. The first modern census of Turkey was

taken in 1927, and because of a probable undercount, the annual rate of just over 2 per cent shown by the census of 1935 could have been exaggerated. Nevertheless, as the Turkish-Cypriot natural increase may have been less than the Greek-Cypriot growth of 1·42 per cent a year between 1881 and 1931, it is possible that the Turkish rate of increase on the island was closer to that of the Greek-Cypriots than of the mainland Turks. Growth in Turkey is shown by the censuses from 1935 on to have been at the following rates (enumerations have been made every five years, but the periods have been selected to coincide as closely as possible with those for which Turkish-Cypriot data are available): 1935–45 – 1·52 per cent a year; 1945–60 – 2·65 per cent; 1960–75 – 2·50 per cent. In the first period, Turks and Turkish Cypriots increased at the same rate; in the next two, the mainland Turkish rate was by far the higher. There is no evidence on which to assess the demographic effects of the disturbed conditions in which the Turkish-Cypriots lived after 1964, but possibly they were unfavourable to population increase, and without them Turkish-Cypriot growth would have been faster than it actually was.

A number of censuses of Greece have been taken, but 'there are both quantitative and qualitative limitations of the data, the most pronounced of which are due to an incomplete count of the universe intended to be measured in each case'.[16] Further, the area of Greece changed from time to time; emigration was substantial at certain periods; and in the early 1920s very large numbers of refugees settled in the country. After analysis of all these factors, Valaoras has estimated the true rates of increase as 1·62 per cent in the 1880s, 1·56 and 1·29 in the two quinquennia of the 1890s, and 0·97 and 0·73 per cent from 1900 to 1905 and from 1905 to 1910 respectively. They then became first 1·26 and then 1·53 per cent in the 1930s, 1·02 in the early 1950s, and some 0·45 per cent in the 1960s. Not only are the effects of, first, emigration and, second, immigration, obvious, but 'the disastrous events which followed the First World War accentuated the decline in the rate of population increase, and may have stopped any increase. Only after the refugee immigration did the rate emerge again into a definitely positive phase . . . this turn of events was mostly due to the more prolific behaviour of the refugees. . . .' Of all these exceptional factors, only one, emigration, had much influence in Cyprus too, so it is perhaps only before 1895 that a fair comparison of growth in the two countries can be made: 1·42 per cent among the Greek-Cypriots, and 1·56 to 1·62 per cent for the Greeks of Greece. All in all, one conclusion may be correct: that the increase of both communities was slower in Cyprus than it was in their respective mainlands.

Cyprus' population growth rate, then, increased steadily from 1881 to 1960, except for an apparent downturn between 1910 and 1930 which may have been exaggerated by some under-enumeration in at least one census. In the last period for which country-wide data are available, 1946–60, natural growth must have reached 2·2 per cent a year – quite a high rate by any standards. The overall trend accorded closely with the pattern of increasing prosperity. The rates for the two main communities differed remarkably, however, Turkish growth being little over a third of that of the Greeks at the outset, but 25 per cent more by 1960. After that year, the Greek rate, already falling slowly, plummeted to a level typical of western Europe; that of the Turkish-Cypriots has remained in doubt for lack of reliable data, although it seems likely that any fall it has experienced has been of lesser extent.

Having traced the new trend of moderate but steady growth since 1881 and the unexpected but very marked differential between Greek and Turkish increase on the island, let us now turn to the contributions made to these processes by the three factors concerned – mortality, fertility and migration.

5

MORTALITY, FERTILITY AND MIGRATION

Mortality

ANNUAL totals of deaths derived from vital registration were published from 1901. The crude death rates calculated from these data – and averaged over three successive years, to reduce the effects of possible late returns – reveal a pattern of increase until about 1923 followed by a fall to implausibly low levels in the 1950s. This pattern will be seen in Table 4 (p. 66).

From year to year the total of registered deaths varied considerably – 3,659 in 1904 and 4,452 in 1905, and 5,058 in 1941 and 6,747 in 1942, for instance. In the 1920s an increase in deaths of 6 per cent over the previous decade accompanied by a 12 per cent growth in population suggested that mortality was falling. However, that suggestion runs contrary to the increase in the official death rate up to 22 per 1,000 persons in 1923, so it is necessary to look more closely to see that at certain times reported deaths soared, particularly in 1918–22, when the annual average was the highest ever recorded over a similar period. Further peaks were reached in 1937 and 1942. It could hardly have been a coincidence that many more cases of malaria than usual were reported in the former of those years. However, before 1942 malaria control had been intensified, and it was reported that in one area at least the disease was no longer of importance. Did some other exceptional cause of death exist? Perhaps a clue may be found in the arrival of refugees from various war zones, many of them emaciated, verminous, short of food and water, and suffering from exhaustion, according to reports from the Medical Department.

As related earlier, the registration system largely collapsed in 1955, so all totals of deaths published subsequently have been estimates. Of course, some deaths were still reported, but as they numbered only 621 in 1958 while the official estimate was 3,450, to cite one example, the element of estimation was large. Even the

63

reported total in 1954, the last of the years when it was thought that registration was fairly complete, was seen later to be deficient. The effect of this inaccuracy was far-reaching. From 1955, the estimates were based on the trends of the last three pre-emergency years, 1952 to 1954, and by 1961 the estimate had sunk to 3,254. However, a different estimate for 1961 made later gave a new figure of 6,206. Since deaths could not conceivably have increased from 3,674 as reported in 1954 to 6,206 seven years later, one figure or the other – or both – were seriously in error. As will be shown, it was the new estimate for 1961 which was more nearly correct; consequently, the 3,674 deaths recorded in 1954 were greatly understated. It is apparent that registration of deaths was more complete early in the century than in the 1950s, so it is not altogether surprising to find exaggerated official claims that Cyprus' death rate was among the lowest in the world – 5·9 in 1961, for instance, while that of the United Kingdom was 11·9.[1] No reason for the unusual deterioration in the registration system before 1955 has been offered officially, and it can only be concluded that the work of the *mukhtars*, which included the registration of births and deaths, became less assiduous.

The series of revised estimates of deaths just mentioned, actually made in the 1970s but backdated to 1961, has been continued up to the present. It purports to apply to the whole island, although the government has received virtually no information about Turkish-Cypriot vital events since 1963. The third highest total of all time was in 1974 – 6,900 deaths. As the average of the preceding and following two years was approximately 6,000, it presumably implies some 900 additional deaths during the coup against President Makarios and the Turkish invasion. The real number of casualties among Cypriots is impossible to assess, as no official figures have been issued and estimates vary greatly. According to one commentator, the casualties resulting from the coup did not exceed 150 dead and 500 wounded – figures difficult to verify, he added, because the Turkish invasion, coming a few days later, confused the issue, but it was certain that no more than 45 national guardsmen, 75 auxiliaries and 20 civilians were killed; the invasion itself caused about 2,000 casualties to the Greeks and roughly the same number to the Turks, and the civilian casualty list was also important.[2] Presumably most of the Greek casualties were of Cypriots, since mainland Greece's forces on the island were small, while the great majority of the Turkish casualties were, from the nature of events, among Turkey's army. But different consequences of the coup have been cited elsewhere, for instance a figure of 3,000 killed, according to a report published in England,[3] while the *Akel News Letter* of January 1977 stated: 'The members of the party and the people's movement that fell during the fascist coup and the Turkish invasion are over 3,000'[4] – implying that in addition to communists, many others died as well. A further report mentions 4,000 to 6,000 killed in the invasion,[5] and another over 6,000 killed.[6] The figure of 1,000 Turkish-Cypriot civilian casualties has been mentioned to the author, in answer to an enquiry. Further, it has been stated authoritatively that more than 2,000 Greek-Cypriots were missing after the fighting;[7] they remain unaccounted for up to today.

According to the Turkish-Cypriot *Statistical Yearbook*, 236 deaths occurred in their zone in 1977, 287 in 1976, and 241 in 1979, implying crude death rates of under 2. Clearly the Turkish-Cypriot vital registration system is not yet functioning efficiently.

Enough data exist to allow the calculation of mortality levels from 1891 to 1971, as described in the Appendix. From them, crude death rates – the number of deaths in any one year per 1,000 of the population – may be derived. Being an easily understood measure of mortality, they are cited here, with a word of warning added: in a population with a large proportion of young people, deaths should be fewer than in a population of the same size containing more elderly people. Hence the rates at different dates may not be strictly comparable, and in Cyprus the population did in fact age over those eighty years, so, other factors excluded, more deaths should be expected by 1971. Despite this reservation, which applies to the official data also, the trend of the rates since the beginning of the century is very clear, as Table 4 shows.

As explained in the Appendix, the calculated rates from 1938 on are based on the answers to census questions, which, it is known from experience elsewhere, some respondents find difficult to answer accurately. Any bias in response is likely to result

TABLE 4: CRUDE DEATH RATES, OFFICIAL AND CALCULATED, 1894–1977

Year	Official	Calculated	Year	Official	Calculated
1894		26	1947	8·8	13·7
1899		25	1952	7·6	10·6
1904	20	20	1957	6·2	10·4
1911	22	20	1962	10·6	8·6
1919	21	19	1967*	9·9	8·2
1929	16	17	1971*	9·6	6·8
1938	13·7	17·7	1977*	9·0	

* Non-Turkish population

in underestimation of mortality. Nevertheless, the pattern of the calculated rates is clearly more plausible than that of the official rates. In the latter, an upsurge of deaths in the decade including the Great War is seen, as well as the surprising deterioration in the registration system from the mid-1930s to 1954. And on looking back, it may be noted that anything approaching complete registration of deaths within a year or so of the inauguration of the system is exceptional and must be seen as a tribute to the efficiency of the local administration.

That the official rate actually exceeded the calculated rate at certain times must cast doubt on the reliability of the latter, and is certainly unusual enough to warrant examination. Comparing the numbers of registered and calculated deaths in the period concerned helps to suggest an explanation (see opposite).

The period 1916–25 was apparently exceptional. A glance at the year-by-year figures shows that particularly large numbers were recorded in 1918 and 1920–22 – as many as 9,924, a record for all time, in 1922, to be followed by a more normal 5,714 in 1923. The 1918 total, 8,024, attracted comment in the *Annual Report* – the increase over the previous year was partly due to the influenza epidemic, but 'it is still somewhat difficult to obtain accurate information as to the causes of death, and consequently to account for variations in the death rates'. Influenza was men-

	Calculated deaths	Registered deaths	Percentage registered
1901–10	51,800	41,923	81
1911–20	55,700	55,797	100
1921–30	57,100	59,016	103
1911–15	27,300	25,359	93
1916–20	28,300	30,438	107
1921–25	27,800	33,324	120
1926–30	29,300	26,692	91

tioned again in 1919 and 1920, and in 1922–23 there were severe epidemics of measles. These references reinforce an obviously reasonable suspicion that worldwide influenza around 1920 took its toll in Cyprus too. Whether the pandemic together with severe malaria in one year and measles in another were enough to account for the exceptional numbers of recorded deaths is not clear, but possibly a precursor to the events of the Second World War also contributed. Refugees in large numbers arrived on the island – a steady influx in 1919 and 1920, 3,000 Armenians in 1921, 2,400 persons including 500 Armenians in 1922, according to the *Annual Report*. Yet, although still more Armenians arrived later in the 1920s, their numbers in the censuses suggest net immigration of about 500 persons between 1911 and 1921 and 2,000 in the following decade – many less than the recorded arrivals. Many of the refugees were of the poorest classes, the *Annual Report* for 1923 observed; a year earlier they had brought smallpox with them, and sixteen deaths resulted. On the basis of such remarks, we may wonder whether many refugees died soon after arrival. In the case of the Armenian newcomers at least, some certainly appeared to be no longer part of the population in 1931, for one reason or another. As it is unlikely that the completeness of death registration suddenly rose to more than 90 per cent, the deaths recorded in 1916–24 should probably be increased by some 10 per cent before the true figures are reached; and we may conclude that the upsurge in mortality was due, in part at least, to the coincidence of the influenza epidemic with measles and particularly serious malaria, as well as the presence of refugees who certainly brought smallpox with them and perhaps other diseases unusual to Cyprus as well.

By way of comparison, the following estimates of crude death rates in Greece and Turkey[8] are cited:

	Greece	Turkey
1935–39	15	35
1945–49	?	28
1955–59	10	18
1965–69	9	13

Cyprus' pattern of mortality since 1931 has obviously been far closer to that of Greece than that of Turkey – a conclusion which is probably valid for Cypriot Turks as well as Cypriot Greeks, although the evidence to prove, or disprove, it is not available.

Totals of deaths under one year of age were published from 1916. Examples of the resulting infant death rates are:

1916–20	139 per 1,000 births
1926–30	151 per 1,000 births
1937–39	128 per 1,000 births
1942–44	122 per 1,000 births
1946–48	68 per 1,000 births
1951–53	56 per 1,000 births

It might be expected that infant deaths, following the overall mortality pattern, were falling by 1926–30. But apparently they were not, and the total in 1922 – the record year for all deaths – was exceeded in both 1928 and 1929. Total, and infant, deaths therefore followed different patterns:

	Total deaths	Infant deaths	Percentage infant in total deaths
1922	9,924	1,502	15
1928	5,235	1,591	30
1929	4,731	1,698	36

The reason for this variation is not clear, but obviously some of the principal causes of infant and of general mortality did not coincide. The halving of the rate in the late 1940s – the likely reasons for which will be mentioned later – is to be noted particularly. However, by now we may expect that these figures are not wholly accurate, and three reasons in particular may be cited. Firstly, total deaths were understated according to our calculations, so the reporting of infant deaths was almost certainly deficient too. Secondly, the divisor in the calculation, the number of registered births, may have been inaccurate. Thirdly, some young children dying could well have been inaccurately classified by age, causing the dividend also to be incorrect – too small rather than too large, probably. Could such errors cancel out, and the calculated rates be, in fact, reasonable? It is possible; but more significant is the likelihood that the three biases – all instances of inaccurate reporting by the public – were consistent over the years. Consequently, the *pattern* of the rates may well be correct, if not their exact dimension. To this, one reservation should be added: as the official death rate was very markedly lower than our calculated rate just before 1955, under-reporting of infant deaths may have been acute at the same time; if that were so, the fall in the rate in the early 1950s shown above was exaggerated. However, when all these points are taken into account, there can be no doubt that infant mortality declined remarkably between 1935 and 1950.

In Turkey, the pattern was entirely different, the infant death rate still being as high as 155 in 1966.[9] In Greece, it was very similar to that of Cyprus, falling from 122 in the early 1930s to 53 in the early 1950s.[10]

After 1955, Cyprus' estimated totals of infant deaths appear to be unreliable. For instance, there were unexplained falls from 714 per year in 1952–4 to 436 per year in 1955–7, and from 327 per year in 1975–6 to 206 per year in 1977–8, and the original estimates of 430 per year for 1967–8 were later revised downwards to 370 per year. Such eccentricities in the series presumably result from imperfect estimation, and are, it must be admitted, hard to fathom, when it is seen that between two of the pairs of years just cited, 1975–6 and 1977–8, the male infant death rate is said to have fallen from 29 to 28, while the female rate dropped from 27 to 13. A decrease from 27 to 13 in a year or so and rates of 28 and 13 for males and females respectively are equally implausible. The latest available figure of 16 in 1979 is, then, almost certainly underestimated, but by how much is impossible to say. Particularly since only the Greek-Cypriot population is in question, the true level in the 1970s could well have approximated to that of Greece, i.e. 24–7.

Reading infant mortality rates from the model life tables (South) calculated earlier to be appropriate gives the following results:

1891–1900	177
1911–20	143
1935–39	138
1947–51	101
1957–60	82
1966–69	63
1970–71	53

Up to about 1946, the rates derived from registration were not dissimilar, but the very marked fall in the former just after 1946 is not reflected here, because a life table sets out the mortality of a population throughout its whole age range. Consequently, no reason is found here for supposing that the pattern of that decline is anything but sound. From 1955 the life table rates may well be more accurate than the registered rates.

After the observation of a Cambridge professor in 1801 that 'there is hardly upon earth a more wretched spot', the island being ridden with pestiferous air and contagion, an official statement in 1881 that the island was generally healthy suggests a great improvement in health in the intervening years. A notable feature of it must have been the disappearance of plague around the middle of the century. Yet different people held differing views. The predecessor of the High Commissioner who reported the island to be salubrious thought the mud and filth of the flooding Pedieos river and the fetid smells of Nicosia-within-the-walls unsuitable enough for the government offices for them to be removed to higher ground some distance away. In the mid-1880s, the Chief Medical Officer made some observations in line with the precaution. Because the towns and villages were usually on the worst possible sites, drainage was very difficult if not impossible, and the streets were reservoirs for all refuse and spare water, he wrote. The dwellings were often below the level of the surrounding ground and were damp; they were low, badly ventilated, and generally overcrowded, and privies and drainage dispersed the most noxious fluvia into the dwellings. Heaps of dirt, manure, and carcasses of dead animals were found in almost every yard and on all waste lands. There was no scavenging system of any sort, and water supplies, although pure at their source, arrived at their destinations polluted. It seems fair to reflect that the more complaisant report came from a professional soldier used to countries where plague and cholera were rife, while the other was that of a medical man who foresaw decades of work before achieving what he regarded as minimal standards. Such speculation apart, detailed information about health conditions and mortality at the time is scarce. It is certain that the authorities were alive to the risks that plague, cholera, and smallpox could be introduced from the mainland, for the *Annual Reports* reiterated that quarantine was strict, and remarks such as one in 1896 that smallpox had been imported from Egypt, with some resulting deaths, were common. But it was stated that in contrast to all the neighbouring countries, Cyprus was entirely free from plague, typhus, and other virulent diseases, thanks to stringent quarantine measures. The latter could not have been easy to maintain, for traffic with those countries was continuous and perhaps considerable – with the Cypriot communities in Egypt, by reason of pilgrimages to the Holy Land, and in search of jobs, to give only three reasons. As early as 1885, the *Annual Report* noted that reapers came over from Anatolia, and Christodoulou observed that as Cyprus experienced labour shortages, workers used to come from Syria, Asia Minor, and even Italy: 'Arrivals of labourers from Latakia were an annual phenomenon until the first world war.'

What the chief causes of mortality were, how they varied and why deaths declined are partly matters of surmise. By 1878 plague had disappeared, we know, and when smallpox, endemic only a few years before, broke out, it was usually imported. Cholera had occurred earlier – the French consul had recently died of it – but now was little mentioned. An early report thought that although phthisis was commonly said not to exist, it was actually far from rare, and when it occurred, it was 'very fatal'. The suspicion was confirmed in 1906, according to the *Annual*

Report: a cause of increasing anxiety was the presence of pulmonary tuberculosis, which in certain crowded areas was constituting a real danger, it stated; and in the mid-1920s phthisis was on a large enough scale for an isolation hospital to be opened, even though the number of cases was said to be uncertain because both sufferers and private medical practitioners were reluctant to report them. Diphtheria was the cause of some deaths in 1896 and 1915, but otherwise was seldom mentioned. Serious epidemics of cerebro-spinal meningitis broke out in 1908 and 1909, when they caused 280 and 546 deaths respectively – 12 per cent of all reported deaths in the latter year – and on a small scale in later years. The second British *Annual Report* observed that there was not much dysentery or diarrhoea, and a few years later typhoid was stated to be much more common in most European towns. In 1906 and 1908 outbreaks of typhoid were reported, but by 1911 either it had taken an increased hold or awareness of it was greater, for 299 cases were reported, and the *Annual Report* commented that the water supply to the towns left much to be desired. In the following year 447 cases of enteric fever were reported, but of a mild type with low mortality. Cases must then have multiplied, for by 1920 enteric fever was included in the short list of prevailing diseases; but in 1924 a marked reduction in its incidence was noted, with further comment that 'the great importance of supplies of pure drinking water from the point of view of public health has been a matter of constant concern to the government, and considerable attention was again paid to the improvement of existing supplies and the provision of supplies where none had hitherto existed'. However, it was reported a few years later that enteric fever and dysentery were on the increase, anti-typhoid inoculations were being offered when enteric fever broke out, and 'the general absence of sanitary latrines and the prevalence of flies make ideal conditions for the spread of enteric fever and dysentery. The increasing popularity of water closets which are not accompanied by proper arrangements for the disposal of liquid sewage is a growing menace to public health' (1929). In 1931 dysentery was on the list of prevalent diseases. An epidemic of typhoid in 1933 resulted in the reporting of 500 cases, and was ascribed to the use of the open yard for the disposal of human excreta, plus a serious drought which caused villagers to dig shallow wells in which the water quickly became polluted. Even more cases were reported in 1943, but by then the sanitation programme was being intensified, and although the 1946 Development Programme mentioned 'the disturbingly high figures for typhoid and similar enteric diseases', the Medical Department was listing typhoid in 1953 as one of the diseases for which preventive measures had been largely successful.

By that time, public health unquestionably benefited from the continuous improvement to domestic water supplies. A scheme for providing every village with a proper supply – fifteen gallons per person daily, plus troughs for watering animals and washing clothes – had been drawn up, to be financed by contributions from London, central funds, and the villages concerned, the last obtaining loans from the Loans Commissioners for the purpose. 'Given some such loan facilities, together with the accumulation of wealth which has occurred in most villages during the war, it should not be beyond the means of the village people to afford the half share proposed.'[11] During 1946 thirty-six villages were connected to piped supplies for the first time. In the next few years, work continued on locating sources, laying pipelines, building storage tanks, and erecting fountains – these being a combination of stand-pipe, trough, and drainage soakpit, of which examples marked with a date in the 1950s are still to be seen, although they have been made redundant by house-to-house supplies. Seventy-seven village systems were completed in 1952, of which twenty-six were new, and it was estimated that 426 of the country's 627 villages were supplied with piped water – a misleading statistic, for if safe water were supplied to two-thirds of the villages, probably 90 per cent or more of the rural population benefited, since it was the larger villages which were supplied first. Those 426 villages increased to 569 by 1962. Within ten years of the end of the war, then, the risk of disease borne through domestic water was virtually eliminated for a very large proportion of the population.

Apart from malaria, the subject of regular comment in official and unofficial reports alike, little consistent theme is to be found here. If phthisis were concealed, no doubt other diseases were too, so while the Medical Department must have known the general state of health – and was highly successful in certain matters such as combating and preventing epidemics – it was certainly unable to obtain complete returns. As well as the remark in 1918 that there was still difficulty in ascertaining the causes of death, it is interesting that the *Annual Report* for 1915 recorded 5,473 deaths, including eleven from typhoid, six each from diphtheria and malaria, and five from meningitis – but did not suggest the causes of the remaining 5,445. The currently prevalent diseases were mentioned from time to time, but not the main causes of death. However, the theme of typhoid, enteric fever, and dysentery seems to have appeared often enough to be of special significance, particularly as procuring domestic water was a constant problem, owing to the dry climate. Water supplies and the incidence of enteric fever were linked in the *Annual Reports*, and if water-borne diseases were in fact an important and continuing cause of mortality up to the 1950s, it would be far from surprising.

The impact of malaria on the population is hard to gauge. In 1930 it accounted for 11 per cent of all cases reported by the government's medical officers, and they were only a small proportion of all the malaria cases occurring, it was stated; in the following year the percentage rose to 18. However, neither figure is informative, for the disease was not notifiable. There were also apparently conflicting reports about malaria. An early High Commissioner stated that the health of the troops left nothing to be desired, yet just previously the Surgeon-General had written that nearly a quarter of his force in Larnaca was in hospital with fever, and that the men of the Paphos detachment 'looked exceedingly ill; even those at their duty, with exceptions which were quite rare, had no strength for active or for any continued exertion'; a fifth of those at Paphos were invalided away, and the daily average of sick amounted to a sixth of those remaining.[12] No doubt the Surgeon-General reported from detailed records, and from his statement, as well as another by a later Governor that one in ten of the troops in Cyprus died of malaria and more than half were always ill,[13] the gravity of malaria for the British forces seems beyond question. But some of the military would have contracted the disease in other countries, and most probably had little immunity to it, so its effects on the British forces and on the Cypriots may have differed. Nevertheless, malaria unquestionably affected the Cypriots themselves very seriously, if less spectacularly – it was a disease which debilitated rather than killed. Baker observed in 1879, for instance, that on the plains many children were extremely delicate and that enlargement of the spleen was common, while Christodoulou thought eighty years later that the transformation brought to the health and well-being of the island by the eradication of malaria deserved to be considered the most important event in Cyprus' modern history. Malaria's effects in Cyprus were probably less than experienced elsewhere, since the local disease was said to be of a mild variety, but 'An intensely malarious locality cannot thrive. The children are wretched, the adults racked with fever, and the whole place shunned whenever possible by the neighbours – gradually it becomes depopulated and untilled, the home only of the most wretched peasants', wrote the leading authority, Sir Ronald Ross, adding that malaria was 'perhaps the most incapacitating disease to which man is liable'. Ross visited Cyprus at the request of the government in 1913. He reported that while malaria on the island was of medium degree, it tended to increase with growing civilisation, extended irrigation, etc., so the spleen rate of 20 per cent was a real public danger – one never knew what it might develop into. Malaria's influence on the death rate was considerable, he thought, particularly on that of infants; it adversely affected not only population growth but the prosperity of the whole island. He recommended preventive measures based on reducing the numbers of mosquitoes and distributing quinine to the public, and they, together with auxiliary measures such as training staff and experimenting with different larvicides, were immediately and vigorously put into effect. Very shortly, good results were observed. In twelve months in 1916–17 only 3,700 cases of malaria were reported, compared with 10,000 in 1912, the spleen rate was no more than 8 per cent, although it rose again later to 13, and the *Annual Report* was able to state that 'with proper precautions, there should be no difficulty in enjoying complete immunity'. The huge task of cleaning and draining streams and marshes, filling in pools – which resulted in the reclamation of 1,000 acres of marshland in ten years – and the oiling of the surfaces of disused wells and stagnant waters was continued methodically. Nevertheless, malaria accounted for 18 per cent of the patients at government hospitals in 1932 – and even so were only a small proportion of all malaria cases. Such was the concern still existing that the first comment in the *Annual Medical and Sanitary Report* usually concerned its incidence, and linked it with the year's rainfall – more rain meant more malaria. Extensive drainage works were continued; a new larvicide, Paris Green, was introduced; the mosquito was studied, with backing from the Rockefeller Foundation, and a new vector discovered. By the end of the 1930s, the measures were showing substantial results; for instance, 215 square miles in the Kyrenia and Tilliria areas had been combed, all the breeding places of the anopheles mosquito located, marked on maps, and subjected to control measures, and shortly afterwards no adult anopheles were to be found there and new cases of malaria were minimal. By 1941, malaria had ceased to be of importance in Tilliria, it was reported, and preventive work was being concentrated on Akrotiri and marsh areas in Nicosia district. However, two years later, malaria was again exceptionally severe, and at the same time quinine was in short supply, doubtless due to the war. A Malaria Board was constituted in 1944, with a work programme comprising thirty-two projects aimed at eliminating mosquito-breeding sites. Then in the next year, the concept of malaria control changed, and eradication finally became feasible through the use of DDT. £20,000 was allocated for a new experimental scheme. Spraying of breeding places and of buildings was meticulously carried out,[14] and as a result of a massive country-wide campaign the numbers of reported cases fell from 7,600 in 1944 to 4,500 in 1946, 2,000 in 1947 and 400 in 1948. The campaign was officially described with singular restraint, the *Annual Report* for its last year limiting its remarks – including the confident expectation that Cyprus would soon be declared malaria-free – to five lines. In 1949 not a single new case was reported, and the island was indeed virtually free of anopheles mosquitoes. The campaign officially ended on 9 January 1950, and what the Director of Medical Services termed 'the biggest enemy Cyprus had ever had' had disappeared. Recalling that as recently as 1945 a military camp had had to be abandoned because of malaria, he commented: 'What a victory, and at a cost of only about 13 shillings per head of the population.' What Ross had called 'that great tyranny which now holds half the world' had disappeared from Cyprus. Through extreme vigilance combined with active precautions, malaria has not been allowed to recur. The danger of its reintroduction from abroad was realised from the outset, and anopheles were actually found on visiting ships and aircraft as early as 1950. The inability of the government to exercise control in areas held by Turkish-Cypriots from 1964 caused concern which has fortunately proved groundless, and today anti-malaria measures are one of the few instances of cooperation between north and south. Twenty-four cases were reported in the north in 1977 and four in 1978; whether they were new or imported is not known. Maintenance work continues today, but the main victory was won thirty years ago, in pioneer and spectacular fashion, over quite a short period, and at a trivial cost.[15]

With malaria wiped out within three years, death rates should have plummeted, it may be thought, but the facts do not quite accord with that thesis. By our calculations, the overall rate fell by about a quarter between 1947 and 1952, but the decline in the infant rate as officially reported occurred just before 1946 rather than after. According to the government's statistics, the average annual deaths prior to and after the eradication campaign numbered:

	All deaths	Infant deaths
1940–45	5,002	1,309
1949–52	4,038	881

However, infant deaths during the three years of the campaign, 1946–8, averaged 1,010 per year – much closer to the later average of 881 than the earlier figure of 1,309. After 1945, then, mortality declined in a marked, but slightly unexpected, pattern. While the reasons for almost any fall in mortality are complex, two in particular were probably significant for Cyprus. Firstly, the energetic anti-malaria measures of the past thirty years had proved successful in certain areas, and consequently the impact on public health of the disappearance of the disease was not as great as it would have been without it. Secondly, malaria incapacitates rather than kills. Because it left its Cypriot victims weak, unfit for work, and particularly prone to other diseases which do kill, the effect of its eradication on the general death rate was not necessarily direct or immediate. However, the effect on infant deaths was more rapid. It was child deaths which were particularly influenced by malaria, Sir Ronald Ross had observed. If only because infants lack the partial immunity to the disease which adults develop, it can hardly be doubted that the reported reduction of infant deaths by a half within a few years was in large part due to the preventive measures and the eradication campaign of the 1940s, taken together.

The public was paying notably increased attention to health, it was reported. In 1955, for instance, the Medical Department observed that to those who had known Cyprus for a mere ten years, the improvement in the physique of the population was clearly apparent; there was now a positive approach to health which was almost non-existent a few years earlier. The new attitude was emphasised by a further remark: 'In the Annual Medical Report for 1913, the Chief Medical Officer makes the following statement: "I regret that the efforts made to popularise the maternity wards of the Central Hospital, Nicosia, have not been successful. There were 13 admissions during the year." The present situation is such that one is almost tempted to wish that efforts to popularise hospital delivery had been less persistent, as it is now extremely difficult to cope with the numbers of expectant mothers who demand accommodation.' Further comment indicated intensification of the new attitude. A generation earlier, the primary concern of the family doctor was physical impoverishment resulting from inadequate nutrition, the newly formed Ministry of Health observed in 1961, but there had been a marked improvement in living standards since the Second World War, together with a better understanding of food values, and the present standard of nutrition, satisfactory on the whole, largely resembled the European pattern. Indeed, the concern of family doctors had moved on from malnutrition to the evils of over-nutrition and overweight in a large proportion of the population. In the following year, the Ministry noted that the care of the elderly was becoming embarrassing, because advances in medical science, improvements in sanitary and environmental conditions, and raised living standards had caused a significant rise in the expectation of life. Further, the new approach to health was not confined to the urban population; although situated in the towns, the general hospitals served mostly people living in rural areas – road communications were good, and the remotest village could be reached by motor in one hour.

Today, although medical and health services in the southern part of the island are overstrained after the loss of the Famagusta and Kyrenia hospitals in 1974 and the Turkish-Cypriot staff ten years earlier, they are conducted with meticulous care. Taking both public and private sectors into account, there were reported to be one doctor per 1,004 inhabitants and one hospital/clinic bed per 160 persons in 1978. In addition to the four general hospitals, twenty-one rural health centres were in operation, each serving an average of some 10,000 people, staffed by one or more doctors, pharmacists, midwives, nurses, community health visitors, and health inspectors, and providing a small number of beds for in-patients as well as out-patient treatment. Patients needing treatment not available in Cyprus are sent to hospitals abroad at government expense – 133 persons in 1978, for instance. Most of those treated in the country by the government's medical services – well over half of all patients, it is estimated – pay either nothing at all or reduced charges. The training given locally is of a high standard, Cypriot nursing and health inspectors' qualifications having been recognised in the United Kingdom for many years. Finding staff is no longer a problem; while only ten nurses were trained in the first six years of independence and the Ministry of Health's annual report called for a change in attitude to nursing as a profession, the newly found freedom for young women to go out to work has taken nursing in its stride. The Turkish-Cypriot zone had one hospital bed per 235 persons approximately, it was reported in 1979. The availability of adequately trained staff there seems to be in some doubt, but it should improve in one respect at least with the recent opening of a nurses' training school. Over 85 per cent of the Turkish-Cypriot population are eligibile for medical care free of charge, the writer was informed in 1980. In the absence of further information about public health and medical services in the north since 1974, it seems fair to suppose that both fall behind those of the south, owing to the need to make something of a new start and to lack of resources, but perhaps not very significantly. Possibly they could fall further behind in future, because the momentum of progress in the government-controlled area has been and remains, exceptional, despite the set-back caused by the 1974 war.

Is it possible to suggest why both the scale and rapidity of the fall in mortality in Cyprus have been exceptional? An article written in 1950, when the statistics gave Cyprus' death rate as one of the lowest in the world – an exaggeration, we now know –

ascribed the improvement in part to the island's sunny climate.[16] We may think it necessary to look for further reasons. The eradication of malaria was certainly of direct importance, and moreover it came at a time of economic and social 'take-off' – the war years both infused Cypriot life with new ideas and left many people substantially better off financially than before. A less obvious reason was undoubtedly the point made by the Medical Department in 1961 that the general hospitals, although situated in the towns, mostly served rural people, and that even the remotest village was only an hour away by car; it was another aspect of the near-fusion of urban and rural life-styles which we have noted in other contexts. In other countries, scarce resources for improving public health are often concentrated on the towns because the returns are greater where population is concentrated; in contrast, Cyprus's compactness, together with the advent of the motor bus, have allowed the whole population to use urban facilities freely. That the rural population has been not only able, but avid, to utilise the most up-to-date medical methods and advice must be due to a number of factors – rapidly rising standards of education, particularly among women, which laid the foundation for receptiveness to new ideas; the introduction of such ideas into public consciousness through the presence of large numbers of foreigners – allied service men – during the war whose health was exceptionally well cared for, and the return of Cypriots after their experience of war service abroad; the intense concern of Cypriots for the welfare of the family and consequently for the health of their children; and, combined with a natural alertness to innovation, a homogeneity of thought in each of the two communities which is perhaps only found in small populations living in circumscribed conditions – in this case a small island – and which facilitates rapid transmission of news and experience. Like Cyprus' remarkable progress in the health field in the last few decades, such a combination of circumstances and timing is, perhaps, hard to find elsewhere.

In summary, a series of plausible mortality levels since 1891 has been calculated, resulting in crude death rates falling steadily to around 1940, then accelerating, and finally reaching the very low level of 7 per 1,000 in the 1970s. The pattern of mortality over the decades derived from vital registration is seen to have been misleading. Reasons for the trend cannot be identified accurately, but the elimination of plague under the Turks and of smallpox must have been important factors. Water-borne diseases were probably a significant factor in mortality up to the Second World War. Immediately after it, the elimination of malaria, to world acclaim, prepared the way for high levels of public health previously unknown to Cyprus. Today, the medical services, both public and private, are of high standard, matching the mood of the population which both demands them and uses them assiduously.

Fertility

Calculating crude birth rates – the number of births in a year per 1,000 population – from the published data of registered births averaged over three-year periods give results which are summarised in Table 5.

TABLE 5: CRUDE BIRTH RATES DERIVED
FROM VITAL REGISTRATION, 1903–78

Year	Total population	Greek Orthodox	Moslem
1903	29·0		
1913	30·8		
1923	27·3		
1931	30·4		
1941	27·3		
1946	31·8		
1954	26·7	26·9	28·8
1960	est. 25·5	est. 26·2	est. 27·2
1966		est. 22·3	
1973		est. 18·3	
1978		est. 19·3	est. 18·0

The totals registered have always varied considerably from year to year – for instance, 8,649 in 1908, 7,965 in 1909 and

8,703 in 1910 – and as they were probably less affected at that
time by upsurges of epidemics and malaria than those of deaths,
the variations could have been a sign that registration did not
function quite consistently. From 1955 on, only estimates are
available, and as related in Chapter 2, some of them were later
revised. It is the latest which are shown in Table 5, the first
estimate for the Greek Orthodox in 1966, for instance, having
been 26.4. Nevertheless, some noteworthy points are apparent,
particularly the steep fall in the rate for the Greek Orthodox since
about 1960, the slightly higher rate for the Moslems in the years
when cross-classification by religion was available, and the even
greater decline in the Moslem rate up to 1978. However, as we
know registration of deaths by the Turkish-Cypriot authorities to
be grossly deficient, it is impossible to assess the accuracy of that
of their births in the absence of any information about the system.
The apparent slight rise in Greek fertility since 1973 is of interest
in a country where natural growth has almost disappeared, but
may or may not be significant, for the exceptional population
movements in 1974 and the following years must have had
demographic effects which, so far at least, are impossible to
assess.

As described in the Appendix, crude birth rates over the same
period have been calculated by the reverse survival method (in
three variations) and, when possible, by differencing the numbers
of children reported born by the same groups of women at
successive censuses. The results are shown in Table 6.

Noting the dissimilarities between the registered and calculated
rates, we must consider whether the latter really are the more
reliable. There is very little doubt that they are, if only because a
registration system in its early years is likely to be incomplete,
while the censuses – the bases for our calculated rates – were
probably quite accurate. There is no reason to doubt that, early in
the British period, the rate was considerably higher than was
revealed by registration, or that the decline shown in Table 6 was
genuine. No reason for an increase in the 1930s is apparent, but
reviewing the registration data for the 1940s and the calculated
rates together suggests strongly that a 'baby boom' occurred in
Cyprus at the end of the Second World War, as it did in other
countries. A few years later, we see once more, registration
became particularly deficient – in Cyprus' terms, that is, because

TABLE 6: CRUDE BIRTH RATES CALCULATED BY REVERSE
SURVIVAL AND DIFFERENCING METHODS, 1894–1970

| | South | Reverse survival | | Differencing |
| | | West | | |
		5-year groups	Single years	
1894	39·1			
1904	36·9			
1914	33·3			
1924	30·3			
1934	33·4	32·6	33·3	
1944	30·1	30·4	29·2	
1948	33·9	32·0	33·4	
1953	30·6	29·7	29·7	29·8
1958	30·2	29·7	29·4	
1965*	21·9	20·9	20·0	17·9
1970*	18·2	17·7	16·7	

* Non-Turkish-Cypriot population

by the standards of many countries it was still good. After 1955 it
was only the censuses which gave good evidence of the fall in
fertility, and no means existed by which the annual estimates
could keep pace with it. Whether the South or West tables give the
more accurate results for Cyprus is investigated in the section of
the Appendix dealing with the balancing equation. Of the rates
obtained by the differencing method, the second appears
unsound – a sign, probably, of some weakness in the 1973
enumeration. All in all, vital registration has given a rather
misleading picture of fertility trends since the system was
established, understating the level in the earliest days, failing to
identify the post-war 'baby boom', and underestimating the
remarkable fall in fertility beginning in about 1959. In particular
it gives the impression that the decline began from about 1948
instead of the 1880s – or earlier.

   Gross reproduction rates since 1950 – the number of daughters
which would be born to a group of women if the group passed

through its reproductive life with the current birth rates applicable to each age group – are shown in the Appendix. They are a sensitive measure, and are therefore commonly used, but being based on vital registration, they are incorrect if registration is deficient. Having estimated the extent of under- and over-registration of births up to 1970, we may revise them (assuming that the deficit, and subsequently the excess, of registered births was distributed among age groups of mothers in the same proportions as the registered births themselves). The corrected series is:

(1946	2·42)
1950	2·18
1960	1·86
1965	1·40*
1970	1·26*

* Non-Turkish-Cypriot population

Here the scale of the remarkable fall in fertility in recent decades is clearly seen.

How that fall lagged behind the decline in the death rate is illustrated in Figure 2.

Hardly any contemporary comment on the likely accuracy of registration data was made, although the *Annual Report* stated in 1914 that it should have improved with the enactment of the Births and Deaths Registration Law. There is little sign that it did. Later, there was a tendency to accept it without demur, *Vital and Migration Statistics* for 1962, for instance, observing that registration since 1900 had been quite reliable. Even Percival seemed surprised on concluding in his 1946 census report that registration of births in the 1920s was deficient. Recently, however, the system's deficiencies have been recognised and efforts made to perfect it, including obtaining the long-term services of a United Nations adviser – an unusual step for a system which has been in existence for eighty years.

The birth rates of Greece and Turkey confirm that fertility levels in Cyprus have been not unlike those of the former country, while Moslem fertility in Cyprus bears little relationship to that of Turkey. According to Valaoras' estimates and later official

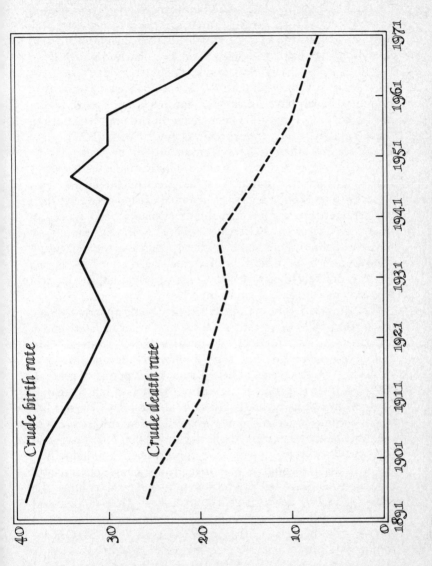

Figure 2. Calculated crude birth and death rates, 1895–1971. (Excludes Turkish-Cypriots after 1964.)

data, the rate in Greece fell from 27·6 in 1935–9 to 15·4 in 1973 – a rather sharper decline than in Cyprus, although starting from almost exactly the same level. Between the Turkish rates in Turkey and Cyprus, however, hardly any resemblance exists, the former ranging from 51 in the mid-1930s (official figure) down to 39·6 in 1974 (United Nations estimate), in contrast to 29 in Cyprus in 1954, 27 in 1960, and a possibly dubious 18 in 1978. Even in 1931, Cyprus' data show, the true Turkish-Cypriot birth rate could hardly have been higher than 36 – lower than the figure for Turkey over forty years later. According to vital registration, then, Turkish fertility in Cyprus was much closer to that of the Greek-Cypriots than to the levels found in Turkey itself.

Two further points may be noted. Firstly, while the Moslems had slightly more children than the Greek Orthodox, at least from 1946 to 1960, a greater differential existed between urban and rural fertility, and it is probable that urbanisation has been an important factor in the fertility decline. Secondly, the classic pattern of the decline noted in the Appendix – the decreasing contribution to total fertility of women aged over 35 – is one which is unlikely to be reversed. Consequently, total fertility will probably not increase again by much.

Why the real decline in Cypriot fertility should apparently have dated from 1890 or so rather than some earlier or later time is impossible to say, for lack of statistics and of contemporary comment and report, but some points of relevance may be suggested. The first years of British rule were a period of general, steady, but slow, progress, as was noted earlier, but thereafter changes in aspects of life likely to influence long-term fertility trends became noticeable. One was the age of marriage; it rose in the case of females, leading to the likelihood that births were not necessarily reduced, but were at least postponed. Internal migration increased – signifying for more and more people not merely a change of residence but of life-style too, as they abandoned the countryside for a new existence in the towns. More marked still was the spread of literacy among young women: of those aged 20–24 – the beginning of their reproductive lives, by Cypriot standards – only 16 per cent were literate in 1911 but as many as 49 per cent in 1931. And during the First World War, Cypriot men left the island to play their part in it, and returned later with both broadened outlooks and more cash in their pockets than their farms had earned for them before 1914, as they did again between 1939 and 1945. That this progress halted in the 1930s is not necessarily surprising, because a decline in fertility does not automatically follow from those influences usually associated with it; they can, indeed, cause an initial increase. Such patterns differ in varying circumstances, and in Cyprus, apparently, conditions existed after 1931 which offset the long-term trend for some twenty years.

Although the decreasing fertility of the last two decades has not gone unnoticed in Cyprus – it is, in fact, obvious within most families – little has been written about its reasons. The 1962 issue of *Vital and Migration Statistics* calculated the ratios of births to females aged 15–44 in 1946 and 1960, and noted that the fall from 142 to 119 per 1,000 was 'mainly due to the heavy emigration of 1960, affecting women in the aged group 15–44'. However, had the more common child/woman ratio (described in the Appendix) been quoted and the *rise* in it observed, an explanation of emigration would actually have been more valid, because the ratio of births to the females present in a particular year is not affected by past emigration. In 1968, the *Demographic Report* gave more cogent reasons – a smaller proportion of females aged 15–44 in the total population; the desire for fewer children, in order to meet the increased needs of the day; and changes in attitude towards religion and towards women's role in the family and society at large., A few years later, the authors of *Lysi* observed that in that Greek-Cypriot village at least, secondary schooling – most of which had to be paid for – was now a necessity except for children destined to take up agricultural occupations, and that dowries for both girls and boys were a serious preoccupation for parents; in consequence, parents chose to have smaller families.

Hoping to enlarge on these explanations and possibly discover others, the author has sought the views of numbers of people in Cyprus – medical men and others observant of life on the island. Most of them would not have realised that emigration could invalidate comparisons of child/woman ratios at different dates or that the proportion of females aged 15–44 in the population had fallen, but the other reasons put forward by the *Demographic Report* were amply confirmed. Better standards of education were linked with the prosperity which began during the war;

then the recession of the late 1950s caused people to husband their resources and spend less on their children. About the same time, a fundamental change in social patterns occurred: whereas professional people previously came from the highest social class, they now sprang from the middle and lower classes as well. The benefits of a good education became obvious to all, almost every family wanted secondary schooling for its children, and very many looked further forward to a university. The traditional determination of parents to do their utmost for their children and the increasing cost of doing so – providing a house for the daughter, a good education for the son, and, when possible, equally good education for the girls as well – was not matched by the money they had available. Better schooling produced its own reaction in time: well-educated women wanted to work after marriage as well as before, and so became less reliant on the traditional interest of rearing children. Among the persons consulted, this train of thought was agreed on unanimously; it is typified by the concise remark of one informant that it is best to have two children, educate them well, and let them live well. Other points of interest were added by individuals. One thought that incentives to have children – allowances, maternity leave and so on – were inadequate today. Two points had a political background: Eoka's violence in the 1950s put many people off having children – to which may be added, presumably, the political and economic uncertainty around 1960 which caused large numbers of people to emigrate; and today, the uncertain political outlook tends to have the same effect. A less orthodox consideration was said to concern Greek-Cypriot morale: after being depressed by the 1974 war and the ensuing flood of refugees from the north, it surged up again, determined to show the world that whereas Turkey used military force, Greek-Cypriots could retaliate with economic strength – in which process there was little time to bring up children!

The change in attitude towards religion mentioned by the *Demographic Report* is less easy to pinpoint. The remark clearly implies that the Church favours larger, rather than smaller, families. However, the attitude of the Orthodox Church of Cyprus to family size may have been uncertain until recently. Enquiry by the author has elicited the authoritative reply that the Church has had no relevant policy, that it was neutral; individual priests, on the other hand, are said to have encouraged large families – after all, the procreation of children is one of the purposes of marriage according to the Church, and not wanting to have children is a ground for divorce. Certainly a number of individuals confirmed the opinion of the *Demographic Report* that decreasing attention to the Church's teachings has helped to bring about a smaller family size, implying that local priests' views had once carried weight. But after being officially neutral, the Synod decided in March 1980 that families with many children should be exempt from paying the usual fees for baptisms, marriages, funerals, and the provision of Church certificates. 'The purpose of this decision of the Church of Cyprus is to relieve large families of financial burdens and at the same time encourage larger families.'[17] When the author asked why such encouragement was now being given for the first time, he was told that the problem of very small families was now occurring for the first time.

The government, on the other hand, continues to maintain a neutral attitude. It does not provide family planning advice or services. A possible change in policy was presaged by the formation in 1979 of two committees, one ministerial and one technical, to study Cypriot fertility – because, the author was informed, the government is interested in raising the birth rate. No report by either committee has been released at the time of writing, nor, it is thought, have their deliberations progressed far. One positive step was taken by the government in 1974 – the liberalisation of the law concerning abortion, which had hitherto been illegal, by means of an amendment to the Criminal Code. The new provision permits the termination of pregnancy in the following circumstances: by a doctor; if the pregnancy was caused by rape; if two doctors consider that if the pregnancy continued, the woman's life would be endangered, or that she or any member of her family would suffer mental or psychological harm, or that the child 'would be subjected to serious physical or mental anomaly'.

A rapid fall in fertility culminating in a level which is low by any standards suggests that Cypriots are aware of the modern means of avoiding conception; and this is generally the case. Contraceptives are easily available, in general their cost presents little or no problem and village people are as conversant with them as the town-dwellers. In addition to contraceptives, abortion could presumably have played a role in the reduction of fertility since 1974, but reluctance to discuss it, together with the fact that most abortions are carried out in private clinics which are not required to make official returns of them, makes it difficult to suggest if its use is widespread. However, some doctors mentioned their own experience of remarkably high proportions both of pregnancies terminated by abortion and of female patients who had had an abortion in the past. It seems, then, that abortion plays a part in today's low level of fertility, but how significant it has been in the decline is impossible to say. A different practice which must have helped to space out births in earlier times may also be noted – the breast-feeding of infants for some three years, as mentioned in *Lysi*. When the author enquired if this had been general, no one doubted it; one doctor told the author that breast-feeding could go on for not merely three but six years, so that some children were being breast-fed while attending school.

Turning to fertility differentials within the population, few informants whose memories went back to 1963 and earlier thought there was much difference in size between Greek and Turkish families in Cyprus. But most knew from their experience that rural families were bigger than those in the towns, and yet stressed that in knowledge of contraceptive methods rural women do not lag behind. It was also mentioned that very many rural women now have their babies in town hospitals and clinics, and firm supporting evidence came from the fact that in the small but apparently well-equipped hospital at Platres, 3,700 feet up in the Troodos mountains, there had not been one childbirth for at least three years when the author visited it in 1980; mothers preferred the facilities offered by Limassol town, thirty miles away. Even the village midwives in the area seldom attended a childbirth, although they give pre- and post-natal care regularly. One doctor's remark typified general comment: nowhere in Cyprus is more than an hour's journey from a hospital, which is a great advantage to the public's health and to maternity services in particular. We may reflect that without the exceptionally close urban–rural relationship which exists in Cyprus, rural fertility would probably be higher today than it actually is – on the lines of the differential found in Greece and Turkey, perhaps – and that the recent overall fall in birthrates is yet another sign of its importance in the island's life.

Finally, a factor thought earlier to have contributed to the rapid fall in mortality has almost certainly affected fertility levels too, if wider experience, notably that of Mauritius and Malta, is to be credited: the existence of a small population in a circum-scribed area. Accompanied in Cyprus by an outstanding capacity for absorbing new ideas and rapidly rising educational standards, it has served to reduce urban–rural social and intellectual differentials to an unusual degree and facilitated the spread of fresh concepts of living in a comparatively very short time.

In conclusion, fertility trends over the last half century are fairly well defined, after examination of the evidence. The marked decline in recent years – sharp enough to arouse some concern – tends to mask the fact that it has been falling since early in this century; it is the accelerated pace which is new, not the fall itself. The main reasons are those associated with the trend to smaller families in other countries – increased prosperity for the indi-vidual, improved education, a greater role for women in the labour force – plus two factors which are exceptionally pro-nounced in Cyprus – diligent and far-sighted concern on the part of parents for their children, and the near fusion of urban and rural life. While all these influences are present in other countries to varying degrees, they have combined in Cyprus to bring about a low fertility level which could hardly have been predicted twenty years ago, with a speed which was equally unforeseen. Many times in the past, Cyprus has experienced small, even negative, population growth while fertility remained high; a low growth rate through low fertility is a new phenomenon in its history, and one which seems, on looking ahead, unlikely to be reversed.

Migration

The official totals of net migration – the balance of immigrants over emigrants – from the inception of records up to 1976 are summarised in Table 7.

As explained in Chapter 2, these figures should be treated with some reserve because of the methods by which they were

TABLE 7: OFFICIAL NET MIGRATION 1920–76

	Net migration	Annual average
1920–30	−7,839	−713
1931–46	−5,417	−349
1946–60	−34,429	−2,374
1961–66	−33,800	−6,760
1967–76	−15,526	−1,553

collected. Nevertheless, those of individual years clearly reflect the exceptional immigration following on the Greek evacuation of Smyrna in 1922 and the outflow in the years after the Treaty of Lausanne of 1923, so it is quite possible that up to the Second World War they were generally valid, at least in broad outline. Certainly no alternative measure of migration at that time exists.[18] As for the post-war years, it is prudent to remember not only the two different bases for the data for some years after 1955 but several individual points such as the following. Emigration of 3,346 persons in 1974 is tabulated, but according to official statements made later, many people left without declaring themselves as emigrants, and a chart in recent *Demographic Reports* actually indicates a net outflow of some 22,000 in that year. In respect of the years 1960–66 a second series issued some years later gave a total of net migration exceeding the figures issued at the time by 12 per cent. The reported numbers of immigrants could not be relied on in the 1970s, it was officially stated, and eventually no report of them at all was made; and with this in mind, we may look back and wonder who the 10,789 immigrants recorded in 1955–60 were, since the civil disturbances of those years hardly encouraged immigration. In one year, apparently, British service families were included in the statistics, although it is likely that they were excluded in the others. Whether returning emigrants were reckoned to be immigrants, then or later, has not always been clear. At that particular period, it seems likely that immigration was overstated.

With all such points in mind and using the data of immigrants and emigrants when they are available rather than those of total arrivals and departures, net migration may be estimated as shown in Table 8. It should be added immediately that despite the margins allowed for uncertain data at particular times, objections to these figures can easily be made: for example, net migration in 1973 is reckoned at −1,312, that being the only figure published, but it was stated at the same time that, according to surveys, immigration had probably exceeded emigration in the past two years, and a chart included in later *Demographic Reports* showed a net inflow in 1973 of over 4,000 persons. All that can be said of these estimates, perhaps, is that when all the evidence is considered, they may be as good as any other.

TABLE 8: ESTIMATED NET MIGRATION, 1901–79

	Estimated net migration	Annual average
1901–10	−4,000	−400
1911–20	−5,000	−500
1921–30	−5,500	−550
1931–46	−5,400	−349
1946–54	−17,200	−2,024
1955–60	−33,000 to −40,000	−5,500 to −6,667
1961–66	−32,000	−5,333
1967–79	−37,000 to −49,000	−2,846 to −3,769
1901–46	−19,900	−442
1946–79	−119,200 to −138,200	−3,506 to −4,065
1901–79	−139,100 to −158,100	−1,783 to −2,027

They exclude movement into and out of the Turkish-occupied area since mid-1974. The only data of relevance to have been issued are of total arrivals and departures in 1976, 1977, and 1978,[19] and the calculated balance of 4,820 departures may be unreliable, as total movements were large – more in each direction in the last year than the whole population – and the balance small. Moreover, the migration resulting from the 1974 hostilities and their aftermath probably began before 1976. An indication of widespread ideas of immigration is found in a report

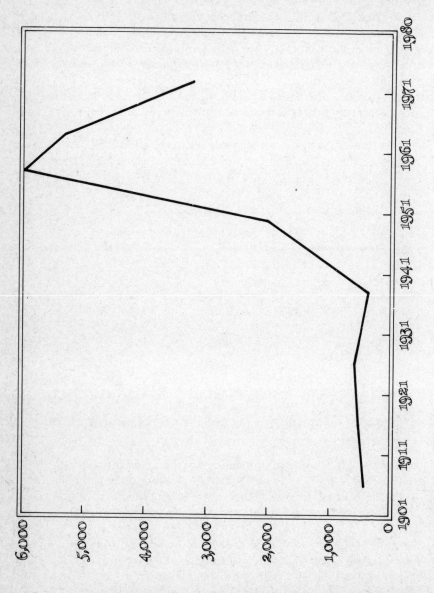

Figure 3. Estimated net emigration annually

of the London *Sunday Times* in September 1976 to the effect that Turkish plans to transplant up to 45,000 mainlanders to Cyprus were being halted after only 18,000 had arrived. Some emigration is commonly thought to have occurred later, but its scale is unknown. So the balance of migration in the Turkish-occupied area since 1974 has probably been on the side of immigration, but it is highly unlikely that good records were kept by an authority which had no experience of them and was not short of other, and probably more pressing, problems.

Another category excluded from the data are the 'temporary workers abroad' from the government-controlled area for whom jobs were arranged in the Gulf states, Libya, and Czechoslovakia during the high unemployment following on 1974, usually with Cypriot companies, and for a year initially. Their number was estimated at 5,700 at the end of 1976 and 4,900 in 1978; it may have totalled 12,000 at one time, and has certainly fallen further recently. It is unlikely that many of the workers will settle in the countries for which they were engaged.

Two types of data available from four other countries may, in theory, be used to check Cyprus' emigration figures: annual immigration returns and census tables. In practice, however, they seem unhelpful. An example is the arrival in Canada over a fourteen-year period of 38 per cent more immigrants from Cyprus than Cyprus' official number of emigrants to Canada; and an even bigger differential is found in the United States' figures over an eleven-year period – 81 per cent. In these countries, as well as Australia, immigrants born in Cyprus in any one year were consistently more than Cyprus' figure of emigrants to the country in question, and in certain years, the difference was large: in 1970, for instance, Australia received 1,212 immigrants born in Cyprus, while Cyprus counted 782 persons emigrating to Australia.

Since the census reports of Great Britain and Australia cite the numbers of persons born in Cyprus, it is possible to make further comparisons – of the additions to the Cyprus-born population in the inter-censal period with the number of immigrants from Cyprus in the same period (Australia only) and with Cyprus' total of emigrants to that country, again in the same period. In the case of Australia, the following results are obtained:

mid-1961–mid-1966:	Australia – immigrants	2,853
	Cyprus – emigrants	2,052
Australia 1966:	additions to the Cyprus-born population since 1961	2,127
mid-1966–mid-1971:	Australia – immigrants	4,631
	Cyprus – emigrants	2,903
Australia 1971:	additions to the Cyprus-born population since 1966	2,564

Some so-far unexplained inconsistency is obvious here, the numbers of immigrants exceeding the other two totals by a considerable margin. Different data in Britain provide results which seem equally puzzling:

1971 census:	persons born in Cyprus first arriving in Britain from 1966 to 1971	11,750
1971 census:	additions to the Cyprus-born population since 1966	13,465
Cyprus – emigrants to Britain 1966–71		6,917

While some difference between the two census figures is to be expected because people may not remember – or know – the year of their first arrival, the lack of correspondence between the British and the Cyprus data is startling.

From these comparisons, three conclusions emerge, it is suggested. First, it is remarkably difficult to obtain good data on migration – as experience has shown in other countries. Among many reasons, the following are relevant to Cyprus: different countries' definitions of immigration and emigration; the unreliability of individual migrant's statements; change of status from visitor to immigrant some time after first arrival; the reluctance of many countries to seek information from persons departing. An assessment of all such factors leaves no doubt that the immigration records of Australia, Canada and the United States are more reliable than Cyprus' emigration data. The second conclusion, then, is that emigration from Cyprus has been understated. It should be added that throughout the world any records at all of emigration are the exception rather than the rule, so this conclusion is not to Cyprus' discredit; on the contrary, Cyprus' effort to document emigrants is laudable and the results are still useful. Thirdly, Cypriots make second-stage migrations – trying out one foreign country, or using it as a stepping stone, before moving on to another. In doing so, they follow a common pattern: for instance, Canada is known to be a staging country for many migrants, to the extent that in the 1960s as many as a third of the United States' immigrants from Canada were second-stage migrants – Cypriots among them, no doubt. The above figures suggest that Australia may be another such country as far as Cypriots are concerned. The United Kingdom and Greece could well be other staging countries.

Despite the conclusion that emigration has been understated, the characteristics of emigrants published from 1955 are of interest, since there is no reason to suspect that certain emigrants are systematically omitted from the data or that the published characteristics are not generally those of all emigrants (with the possible exception of those who left in 1974). A wide range of detail is given – sex, age, race, occupation, district of usual residence, and country of destination. Some of these characteristics will be cited in the following paragraphs.

Early in the century, population growth was not particularly fast compared with many other countries, so what was it that caused continuous emigration? It was Christodoulou's view that modern emigration began with the drought of 1902. Under the Turkish regime, movement to and from the neighbouring countries was probably commonplace and on a large scale, as we have seen. Whether it came to a halt between 1878 and 1902, as Christodoulou's unexpectedly precise date might imply, is not known, but it could at least have slackened. In any case, the implication in Christodoulou's remark that modern emigration had its origins in the poverty of the countryside has always been accepted, for instance by the 1946 census report, and by an informant who told the author that for most people the objective was to leave the Cyprus countryside, and that consequently emigration was merely an extension of the rural-to-urban movement. Rural poverty existed as an apparently permanent condition up to the 1930s. In other countries the rural poor might have crowded into the towns, creating a pool of unemployed living in slums; in Cyprus, however, this hardly happened, for reasons including the family ties which kept the jobless or otherwise unprofitable family members at home and saved them from an uncertain future in the towns, as well as the opportunities to move to more distant destinations such as the United States. Once a few emigrants settled anywhere satisfactorily, word spread, and others followed. In the composition of the flow, family and village connections have been an important factor; hence the existence in the countries of settlement of clubs associated with certain Cypriot villages such as Lefkara and Yialousa.

'Emigration is confined for the most part to the male sex,' stated the 1931 census report. It was a feature which was not to endure, *Vital and Migration Statistics* for 1962 observing, 'Generally speaking, emigration from Cyprus is by family, either the family leaving as a group or one member of the family following another in emigrating to complete the family, members of which have already emigrated.' When reviewing the sex ratios available from 1955 on, three different periods can be distinguished: 1955–57, when males and females were in roughly equal numbers; 1958–62, when males predominated by about 5 : 4; and 1963–79, when their numbers were fewer by about 4 : 5. The radical change in the proportions of males and females between 1931 and 1955 is easily understandable, but what caused the further variations in the following years? The years 1959 to 1962, and to a lesser extent 1958, were periods of high emigration and it was at such times that males predominated. When urgency arises, it is natural that men lead the way in migration, leaving wives and families behind until they find work and a new home. Although 5,000 more men than women emigrated in 1958–62, in the following years an excess of women compensated for that imbalance – as few as 731 males per 1,000 females by 1965. In every succeeding year up to the present – except 1974, possibly – female emigrants have outnumbered males. Overall, however, the official comment of 1962 that emigration from Cyprus was generally by family has now been good for some thirty years.

By contrast, the age pattern of emigrants since 1955 has not been that of Cypriots in general, comprising many more people in the early working ages and fewer children and persons aged 45 and over. A comparison of their age distribution with that of the total population in 1960 and of the enumerated population in 1973 follows:

	Emigrants 1955–79	Population	
		1960	1973
	(percentages)		
0–14	25	37	29
15–29	42	23	27
30–44	20	17	17
45 and over	13	23	27
	100	100	100

About 40 per cent of the general population, but 60 per cent of the emigrants, were in the prime working ages.

After 1922 most of the immigrants must have been Greeks and after 1923 most of the emigrants Turks, but there were no other indications of the racial composition of the emigrants before 1955, although a strong suspicion that it included a disproportionately large number of Turks up to 1930 is mentioned in Chapter 4. From 1955 to 1973 is was almost exactly that of the total population – 77 per cent Greek-Cypriot and 18 per cent Turkish-Cypriot. In general the proportion of the latter increased towards the end of the period, amounting to 29 per cent in 1970–73, the data state. In view of the abnormal conditions after 1963, it may perhaps be questioned whether the reported numbers of Turkish-Cypriots emigrating were correct, as that community lived largely in isolation from the island's government.

No confirmation of the racial composition is found in the list of emigrants' destinations, for from 1955 to 1974 Greece and Turkey hardly featured in it. In the early days, most of those leaving went to Egypt, where there were flourishing Cypriot communities in Alexandria, Cairo, and Port Said, and others to Greece, the United States – where the intake was discouraged by restrictions in the early 1920s – and the United Kingdom. By the 1930s, some were finding employment in the Congo and other parts of central Africa. At one point, the Royal Mail Steam Packet Co. organised migration to the Argentine; it failed after a short time, because wages there were found to be low compared with the cost of living. After 1955, the United Kingdom clearly headed the list of destinations; over three-quarters of the emigrants from 1955 to 1973 went there, and as many as 92 per cent in the peak years 1960–61. Three reasons for this preference were offered by the *Demographic Report* in the late 1960s: a big Cyprus community was already established there, thus offering a foothold to newcomers; moving to Britain was facilitated by Cyprus' membership of the Commonwealth; and the strong attachment of Cypriots to the United Kingdom as the island's last ruler. In retrospect, we may add the widespread use of the English language in Cyprus, and a particular regard for the education their children would receive there. A further 10 per cent went to Australia – for some of the same reasons, presumably – and 5 per cent to North America, thus renewing on a small scale the outflow to the United States occurring before 1922. By contrast, less than 1 per cent went to Greece, and only a third of 1 per cent to Turkey, according to the records. Although exact figures were not issued, more Cypriots probably emigrated to central Africa than to Greece and Turkey combined.

Since records of the large emigration in the second half of 1974 were not kept, the destinations then are not known, but since 1975 a quite different pattern of receiving countries has emerged:

	Emigrants' destinations	
	1955–73	1975–79 (excluding Turkish-Cypriots)
	(percentages)	
United Kingdom	77	15
Australia	10	36
North America	5	18
Greece	0.9	17
Turkey	0.3	–
Other	6.8	14
	100	100

The contrast is clear – a very restricted flow to Britain after 1975, the replacement of Britain by Australia as the main destination, and the emergence of Greece for the first time, at least for several decades, as a receiving country. Opinion in Cyprus suggests that the new pattern is mainly due to Britain's limitation of settlers from Cyprus, and that, without it, Britain would still be by far the most popular destination.

According to the data, limited to the years 1962 to 1973, the six districts provided emigrants roughly in proportion to their populations. However, the more significant point was still that emigrants came from the countryside. There are no statistics to support this contention, but comment leaves the point in no doubt: for instance, the government's London representative recorded it exactly in 1952, and Christodoulou wrote seven years later that emigration was largely a rural phenomenon, and that while it affected nearly every village, some in particular lost considerable proportions of their populations, for instance Lefkara, and others in the Karpas peninsula and near Paphos.

It follows that emigrants were not among the best-educated and most skilled people in Cyprus – considerations which must have affected their prospects for the future, as the government's representative in London emphasised several times only twenty-five years ago. Cypriot students' greatest difficulty in the United Kingdom was poor knowledge of English, and they had to spend the first twelve to eighteen months learning the language, he reported; people lacking adequate knowledge of English should be discouraged from coming to the United Kingdom, as it was difficult for them to find satisfactory employment; and just before independence, the great majority of Cypriot immigrants had a low standard of literacy and very few had any knowledge of English, so it was rather difficult to fit them into an industrialised society. It was a characteristic which has changed in recent years.

Surprisingly, emigrants' occupations, published from 1962, were not those of country-dwellers, only 5 per cent of the economically active emigrants over a twelve-year period being reported as farmers, while 12 per cent were service workers and 63 per cent process, production, and transport workers. Two reasons for this anomaly are suggested. People about to work in industrialised countries would probably not say that they were farmers, for fear of jeopardising their future prospects. Secondly, many workers having urban occupations still lived in their villages. When the occupational structure of working emigrants is compared with that of the whole working population, viz.:

	Emigrants 1962–73	Population 1960
Farmers	5	39
Process, production, transport workers	63	32
Other workers	32	29
	100	100

a misleading impression may be gained, for despite the tiny proportion of emigrant farmers, it was still the rural, rather than the urban, areas which were losing their population. One notable change in the pattern of emigrants' economic activity has occurred recently. Up to 1973, only 3 or 4 per cent of working emigrants were in the professional and technical category, but from 1975 that percentage rose first to 10 and then to 20 in 1978. Restrictive regulations in other countries are reflected here, as professional and well-qualified people have been permitted to immigrate, but not others. Within Cyprus, unemployment among such persons appeared, so some began to emigrate; when qualified teachers, for instance, were forced to queue for jobs in Cyprus, some naturally looked for work abroad.

What work Cypriots actually do in their countries of adoption is not recorded, but the government's representative in London in the 1950s was probably well-informed in saying that many worked in shoe-making and tailoring, women doing particularly well as seamstresses and machinists, and that five hundred restaurants and cafés, including some of the best in London, and sixty hairdressing shops were owned by Cypriots. Since then, the range of occupations has widened to include many of the professions, but one aspect of Cypriots' economic activity in England has probably not changed: a strong preference for self-employment or small family enterprise.

Return migration – the return of former emigrants – could obviously have been on a significant scale, and have affected population growth. So little reference to it has been made that we may wonder whether it was so commonplace as to merit no comment or small enough to pass unnoticed. On the whole, the latter alternative is the more likely. Earlier family interchange with Egypt, Anatolia, or even Greece apart, it seems improbable that many rural Cypriots who left their villages for lack of work ever returned from other countries – except central Africa, probably – either to the villages which would not be able to employ their children in the future, or to the towns where job opportunities were also few. The lack of information is due to the principle that a Cypriot may always return to Cyprus without question. But some inconsistency here is suggested by *Vital and Migration Statistics 1962*, which stated that the immigrants were almost all persons of Cypriot origin who had emigrated and were returning to Cyprus to retire. (However, a tabulation showed only 16 per cent of the 1962 immigrants to be aged 50 or over, that is to say of anything like retirement age.) As ten years later *Tourism, Migration and Travel Statistics* was reporting that there were no reliable data on immigration, we may safely conclude that good statistics of return migration have never existed. Consequently, opinions on the point which the writer has gathered in Cyprus as well as in England and the United States are of interest. They do nothing to contradict the report of the government's representative in London in 1953 that 'normally there is no return movement of Cypriots, although every year a number go to the Colony on short visits'. Confirming that very few emigrants ever return, one informant told the author that a few old people come home to die – but that others leave the island to spend their final years with their children overseas. Another mentioned some small return migration from the United States, which turned into a second migration when the migrants found that conditions at home were not just how they remembered them. Yet another drew attention to a contrast concerning Australia: many Greek emigrants return, so a sizeable Greek–Australian community has grown up in Athens; Cypriots, on the other hand, do not come back. It appears, then, that return migration is probably very small indeed. To this conclusion, three reservations must be added. Firstly, about 1949 the government assisted the repatriation from Egypt of Cypriots who, even though long established, were likely to become destitute. Secondly, the writer has been told that not many emigrants remain in central Africa. Thirdly, the extent to which emigrants in 1974 have returned is as little known as the numbers who emigrated – but we may suppose that those going to Greece have found it easier to return home when an opportunity presented itself than emigrants to, say, Australia.

In the absence of data about return migration, it is tempting to make calculations which include the commonly cited numbers of Cypriots in foreign countries which were mentioned in Chapter 2. However, they are unreliable. Ambiguity in the definition of 'Cypriot' can, in fact, be misleading, as for instance when a writer claimed a few years ago that Cypriots in Great Britain numbered about 120,000 or a fifth of all Cypriots everywhere – a claim based, presumably, on the official estimate of 620,000 persons in Cyprus, but overlooking the point that different definitions were being used. His mention of 15–20,000 Cypriots in Australia, although a recent census had recorded 10,700 persons born in Cyprus, was equally imprecise. The author was told recently in New York of 45,000 Cypriots in the United States, yet the official number of emigrants to that country since 1955 is under 4,500 and the true figure perhaps double that number. Even the government's representative in London in the 1950s, who must have been as well informed as anyone, was probably inaccurate in estimating some 18,000 Cypriot residents in Britain in 1950 and at least 60,000 only seven years later. The most likely such estimate is Oakley's in 1978 – that Cypriots in Britain numbered about 110,000, including 25,000 children born locally to immigrant parents. The figure accords reasonably well with detail from Britain's 1971 census – that 73,295 persons had been born in Cyprus, and that both parents of 9,700 had been born in the British Isles – implying that the latter were the children of British service men; consequently, about 64,000 had been born in Cyprus of Cypriot origin. In case that number seems small in comparison with 110,000 in 1978, a remark made by a London Cypriot to the author may be added: that many Cypriots in England who had been born in Cyprus would unquestionably fail to state that fact on a census form.

Immigration has been the exception rather than the rule. Some immigrants arrived in the earliest days of British rule: Percival, for instance, recorded that 'during the early years of the occupation there were certainly numbers of immigrants from the Ottoman empire'. Some came from Malta too, but only briefly. Unemployment there was severe in 1878, some Maltese made their own way to Cyprus in the expectation of working for the British forces, and the two governments made an agreement in 1880 by which Maltese would be settled in selected, healthy areas at the cost of the Malta government. By that time, however, nine Maltese families had reached Cyprus under the aegis of a private entrepreneur, who had chosen an *un*healthy site near Larnaca for his settlement; all of them caught malaria, and their repatriation caused such a furore in Malta that the governments dropped the settlement plan. Thoughts in later years of reviving it came to nothing, because by then Cyprus's fertile land had been taken up. Once that early inflow subsided – and we may infer from the census figures that either it was small or numbers of the immigrants soon left again – the feeling generally was that expressed by the *Annual Report*: no large field for immigrants existed. Only at two periods did sizeable numbers of people arrive – Armenian refugees in the early 1920s, and, following the Greek evacuation of Smyrna in 1922, more refugees of a variety of races, who were reported to number 2,400 in that year and probably totalled more eventually. Some of them, including Greeks and Maltese, moved on again; many Armenians, on the other hand, stayed in Cyprus. Earlier, there had been two attempts at organised immigration, both of which failed. Over 1,000 Dukhobors from Russia were introduced as settlers by the Committee of Friends in 1898, but, finding themselves unused to a Mediterranean climate, moved on to join their co-religionists in Canada. And in 1900, an advance party of Jewish refugees from eastern Europe arrived; they foresaw snags in the agricultural work planned for them, and left again without the main contingent ever being seen.

The government has maintained a *laissez-faire* policy towards migration, intervening only when special need arose. There was indeed, no call for it to do otherwise. Before the second war, national population policies were not in vogue; and in any case, with emigration regularly removing some of the surplus rural population but not enough to cause misgivings about the future,

105

the government could hardly have done better if it had tried. When a few emigrants were unable to find jobs and homes abroad, and were repatriated at public expense, the government limited emigration for a time to persons holding a promise of employment. Intervention of a different kind followed the Treaty of Lausanne in 1923, which concluded Turkish participation in the Great War. Cyprus was annexed by Britain, and Cypriots were given the option of retaining their Turkish nationality and leaving the island, or of acquiring British nationality. The first alternative was practicable only for Turkish-Cypriots, and their reaction was mixed. Some accepted, but within a few months a representative of the community told the Legislative Council: 'Certain persons of the Moslem section of the population had been led to believe that they would live in a fool's paradise if they emigrated to Asia Minor. These unfortunate people had sold all their belongings in Cyprus before emigrating and now returned to the Island absolutely penniless . . . they were a burden on the Government and on the community. . . .' Some 5,000 persons emigrated to Anatolia between 1924 and 1928, but it is not known how many eventually returned. Many others neither opted for British nationality nor left the island, and the government soon had to make a special arrangement to naturalise them. A requirement of sponsorship was imposed in the 1930s on emigrants to Britain, again to safeguard the individual against unemployment and destitution there and the government against a liability for repatriating him; in 1958, a particularly large number of 'affidavits of support' were made, guaranteeing 5,761 adults and 1,666 minors. Although Cyprus did not encourage emigration, it is noteworthy that when the *Annual Report* commented on the subject, it showed no concern at the continuous outflow. Similarly, *Vital and Migration Statistics* in 1962 appeared unperturbed at the loss of 18,000 persons – 3 per cent of the population – in the first two years of independence. Other cases of official intervention have been the assistance to Cypriots returning from Egypt mentioned earlier, and restrictions imposed by the government and the Turkish-Cypriot authorities on emigration after 1974 – the requirement that young men complete national service first, and the introduction of foreign currency allowances. Such exceptional interventions apart, Cyprus has been satisfied with what a Cypriot writer has termed the relatively unique possibility of exporting its surplus labour in significant proportions.

In summary, emigration has been on a scale large enough to exert a marked effect on population growth, reducing it by 20 per cent between 1946 and 1960, for instance. It used to be primarily a movement of young males from rural areas, but has tended to become one of families, and now includes numbers of professional and technical workers for the first time. The list of destinations has changed, Australia replacing the United Kingdom as the first choice. Return migrants cannot be traced statistically, but their numbers have almost certainly been insignificant, except in respect of people who left during the 1974 crisis. An important effect of emigration has been to reduce both the unemployment which would otherwise have become a mark of rural life and the growth of urban slums which it would have helped to create.

6

OTHER DEMOGRAPHIC CHARACTERISTICS

A VARIETY of characteristics have been tabulated in the census reports. Some of the detail is of little interest today, and many tables were the less useful for lack of cross-classification by age. Others, however, recorded valuable information which was not available from any other source.

Sex

Each census up to 1921 recorded a small excess of males in the population. In the first four enumerations, it was about 1,040 males per 1,000 females; in 1921, the excess almost disappeared, and by 1931 it turned into a small deficit. Was the changing pattern due, perhaps, to improving standards of enumeration, or was the proportion of males in the population really decreasing? Useful evidence is found in the ratios of the urban and rural populations and of the Greek Orthodox and Moslem communities. They are included in Table 9.

In general the trends form plausible patterns. Rural to urban migration is clearly indicated; growing pressure on agricultural land combined with increasing opportunities in the towns for earning cash wages have prompted a continuous movement away from the countryside in which young men predominated, particularly in the earlier decades. Consequently, differentials of forty or more permillage points in the urban and rural ratios were found consistently up to 1960. Reasons for their disappearance by 1973 are not immediately obvious. A slackening of the pace of urbanisation after 1946 might have been one, but in fact the pace increased. The change in 1973 to a *de jure* enumeration should not have influenced the point. So other factors must have exerted an influence – for instance, that in internal migration, as in emigration, the sexes become better balanced. Reasons for such a change could have included a new aspect of population movement after 1955 – the need to seek physical security amid civil

TABLE 9: NUMBERS OF MALES PER 1,000 FEMALES IN
CYPRUS, URBAN AND RURAL AREAS, GREEK
ORTHODOX AND MOSLEM (GREEK-CYPRIOT AND
TURKISH-CYPRIOT) COMMUNITIES, 1881–1976

Census of	Cyprus	Urban	Rural	Greek Orthodox	Moslem
1881	1,037	1,106	1,030	1,023	1,068
1911	1,035	1,089	1,025	1,020	1,080
1931	986	1,023	978	971	1,034
1946	978	1,031	968	971	1,006
1960	967	991	955	964	974
1973		978*	980*	979	
1976				998	977 (1978)

* Excluding Turkish-Cypriots

disturbances, in which circumstances men do not leave their families behind; new effects of the urban 'pull' on women, as growing numbers of girls with secondary education looked for jobs in offices and shops; and the rapid growth of the towns' suburbs, providing housing for families rather than for single men.

While the ratio in the Orthodox community fell to less than parity by 1931, a majority of males was maintained among the Moslems for another twenty years. More than one explanation of this contrast can be suggested – for instance, reluctance among Moslem families to have their younger womenfolk listed. Unfortunately no cross-classification by age is available to show whether it was young girls in particular who were short. However, it is also clear that the Moslem ratios underwent just as marked a change after 1911 as those of the Greeks, falling equally rapidly. Whether the Great War had some adverse effect on the stability of the Moslem population – even though Turkish men hardly left Cyprus to join the allied war effort, as many Greeks did – is not clear, but in the 1920s, certainly, there was emigration to Turkey. Had this movement followed the common pattern of young men leaving in search of work, the Moslem ratio would have dipped below parity. As it was still 1,034 in 1931, we may conclude that the emigration was rather one of families; even, possibly, of older people who had established ties with, and particular affection for, Turkey. Here is a suggestion that the Greek Orthodox and Moslem emigrations of the 1920s may have differed radically in composition. The continued fall in the Moslem ratio after 1946 could have been caused by a further excess of males among emigrants, or by more accurate enumeration of females in successive censuses, or by both factors in combination. The published figure for 1978, whether accurate or not, can hardly be of long-term significance in view of the recent abnormal population movements which may not have ended yet.

What caused the upturn in the Greek ratio after 1960? Firstly, because of the change to the *de jure* principle in 1973, persons studying or visiting abroad were included. Allowing for students, business men, and other travellers, perhaps 2,000 more men than women outside Cyprus were enumerated; had they been omitted, the ratio would have been 973, not 979 – still a reversal of the former trend. A more important factor, probably, was one mentioned earlier – that emigrants were comprising nearly equal numbers of men and women. Consequently, the continuing emigration no longer removed much larger numbers of men than women from the population – a point clearly seen when the sex ratios in age groups are examined later. The new trend was such that by 1976 virtual parity was reported again.

Examination of the ratios in districts – not reproduced here – shows three firm trends: in Kyrenia and Paphos the ratio was always lower than in the country generally, while in Limassol it was always higher. Such figures accord with the conclusion to be drawn later that migration away from the former districts and into the latter has been quite consistent. While only broad trends can thus be discerned because, unlike the provinces of France or the English counties, Cyprus' districts are few in number and, of all the movements made, many must have been within the district, ratios of 917 and 946 in Kyrenia and Paphos districts respectively in 1931, to give one example, were evidence enough of outflows which must have been active for at least fifty years. Subsequently, district differentials have tended to even out, with one notable exception, Paphos, where the 939 and 937 males per 1,000 females found in 1960 and 1973 respectively were almost the lowest ever found in Cyprus, and were apparently still falling. Because out-migration was continuing on a large scale, the Paphos population of 1976 totalled little more than in 1931. In this process, an odd feature appeared – a higher ratio of men in Paphos town in 1960 than in any other urban area – 1,067. This phenonemon was not a sign of new jobs in industry or trade – rather the contrary; it was due in part, perhaps, to the recent civil disturbances, and in part to the function of the town as a staging point for rural migrants moving to Limassol and elsewhere. In the villages, the ratio of 918 probably meant that among *adults* it was little more than 600, i.e. there were no more than six men for every ten women.

The last twenty years, then, have seen a notable change in the trend of the sex structure of the population. Because the particular emphasis on males among emigrants has eased, the decline in the masculinity ratio has halted; and in the towns, women are in a majority, almost certainly for the first time in Cyprus' history. In the latter respect, Cyprus is beginning to resemble the countries of western Europe, but the former feature is unusual in signifying not that emigration has ceased, but that it no longer has much effect on the composition by sex of the population remaining at home.

Age

Although age can be difficult to ascertain through censuses, the five-year groups given in Cyprus' published tables appear not implausible, with a few exceptions. Certainly there were a few seeming irregularities; for example, the numbers in the 5–9 group exceeded those aged 0–4 in 1921 and 1931, and the 40–44 and 50–54 groups were larger than the immediately preceding ones. As the former irregularity had not occurred earlier, we should not overlook the possibility that, in 1921 at least, the youngest group really was reduced in size – possibly by the absence of some males from Cyprus on war service. The same phenomenon reappeared in 1973, but was then caused by the fall in fertility of the later 1960s. It seems, then, that in view of the irregular sizes of the two youngest groups, the observation of the United Nations that 'the numbers of children aged 5–9 as reported in the census can ordinarily be accepted' was not always valid for Cyprus. The second irregularity – the excessive size of the 40–44 and 50–54 groups – was repeated regularly, and was due, we may assume, to a preference by respondents to the census question for the exact ages 40 and 50. The 60–64 group was affected similarly; but, curiously, age 70 appeared to be less popular. Despite such eccentricities – by no means unique to Cyprus – the general pattern of age shown by the censuses has appeared reasonable, and, furthermore, consistent.

The distribution of the population in broad age groups at selected censuses since 1981 is shown in Table 10. Some minor irregularities in 1881 might have been due to unusual circumstances – particularly erratic age-reporting, perhaps, or recent emigration, either temporary or permanent; they led to a proportion aged 60 and over which seems implausibly high and possibly to an over-large proportion aged under 15 – 385 per

TABLE 10: AGE DISTRIBUTION, 1881–1976
(PERMILLAGES)

	0–4	5–14	15–44	45–59	60 and over
1881	139	246	416	105	94
1911	134	239	435	112	80
1931	113	221	458	124	84
1946	123	215	440	127	95
1960	131	236	407	131	95
Greek Orthodox					
1960	125	237	401	136	101
1976	77	178	469	133	143
Moslem					
1960	145	252	401	120	82
(1978	81	214	448	122	135)
Urban					
1973*	85	193	471	139	112
Rural					
1973*	86	210	421	129	154

* Non-Turkish-Cypriot population

1,000. Fifty years later a fundamental change in the age pattern was clearly taking place: the population was ageing, and only 334 per 1,000 were reported to be less than 15. The impetus to this new trend apparently dated from some time before 1921.

Since emigration has always been concentrated in the working ages to a greater or lesser degree, the age structure of the enumerated populations was bound to be affected by it. But it is sometimes partially obscured by a commonly found bias, the preference of young women for ages in the central years of child-bearing. Because of it, an excess of females between 20 or 25 and 35 was always likely in Cyprus. Were the detail of single years available, the role of biased reporting in the years of child-bearing would be clearer, but as it is, it is useful to look at the numbers of males per 1,000 females in broader age groups:

	1881	1901	1921	1931
10–19	1,042	1,048	1,007	1,002
20–29	959	974	904	889
30–39	1,012	1,058	997	972
40–49	1,129	1,066	1,049	967

The arrangement serves to eliminate one likely irregularity, the common preference for ages ending in 0, 5 and 8, because all the terminal digits are included in each group; it does not, however, circumvent that of young women for the central child-bearing years since one of the new groups comprises them all. Whatever the virtues and weaknesses of the new arrangement, it clearly indicates a marked deficiency of young men in each census year, and once more we see emigration as the obvious explanation.

After noting that the population was becoming older, only 334 persons per 1,000 being under 15 in 1931, we can also see an inconsistent trend: while the older age groups continued to grow proportionately, the size of the younger groups increased too. In 1960 as many as 367 persons per 1,000 were under 15. Two contradictory influences were at work simultaneously for a few years. The increasing proportion of the elderly is likely to continue – since the over-60s in the United Kingdom, to cite one

113

example abroad, have recently amounted to nearly a fifth of the total, Cyprus' population, with less than 150 per 1,000 in that age group, can obviously age for some time yet – but the growing proportion of children between 1931 and 1960 seems less easy to understand. The reasons for it have actually been noted previously, in different contexts. The undercount of children in 1931 was large enough to imply a true decrease, not an increase, in their proportion by 1946. Only the period 1946–60 was exceptional, and it was then that the 'baby boom' occurred. By 1960 fertility and natural growth were declining, and the result is reflected in the under–15s enumerated in 1973 – a much lower proportion, probably, than ever before, although not as small as in 1976. The fall from 362 to 225 per 1,000 in sixteen years found among the Greek Cypriots would be remarkable anywhere.

Between the sections of the population for which separate data exist, clear differentials can be seen. In both 1946 and 1960 there were more children among the Moslems than the Greeks, and in compensation, a considerably smaller proportion of the elderly; and those differentials increased during the fourteen-year period. Between the urban and rural populations the variations were smaller, but one in particular was of significance – the increase from 109 to 154 per 1,000 of those aged 60 and over in the rural areas between 1960 and 1973. We may suppose that in many more distant villages, outside commuting distance of the towns, one or more in every five persons can now be 60 years old or over. The remark made to the author in Platres that only the elderly live in the nearby villages was doubtless an exaggeration, but it did point to the unwelcome change taking place in the life of what were balanced village communities not long ago.

The median age of the population – the age of the person who has half the population older and half younger than himself – is a rough indicator of the ageing process. In 1931 it was about 23·2 years; in 1946 23·7 years; and in 1960, 22 years. Having varied little since 1881, it then rose to 27·4 years in 1976.

In Greece, the age structure in 1920 and 1928 was not dissimilar to that of Cyprus, although Greece's deficit of males extended up to 45 rather than 35 years and was much more marked. In 1920, no more than 829 and 817 males per 1,000 females were enumerated in the groups 25–29 and 30–34 respectively – figures which were not mere aberrations of the census, since similar ratios were found in the same cohorts eight years later. They were due, no doubt, to the Great War and the subsequent upheavals in the Balkans. However, despite such events and their demographic consequences in Greece, the sex–age structure of that country and Cyprus were of like pattern overall. The position in later years is indicated by the following summary:

		Proportion aged under 15
Greece	1940	330 per 1,000 persons
	1970	249 per 1,000 persons
Turkey	1935	414 per 1,000 persons
	1970	418 per 1,000 persons

In Greece and Cyprus the trends have remained close to each other, but once again the contrast between the demographic progress of mainland Turkey and the small group of Turks living on Cyprus is very marked.

Marital status

The proportions of persons aged 15 and over who had never married or were married, widowed, or divorced according to the censuses are shown in Table 11.

Between 1901 and 1931 the proportions among males remained steady, but among women a change of some significance occurred – the percentage of the unmarried rose by four points. Clearly, the age at which girls married was rising; at the same time, the gap between the age at marriage of men and women was decreasing. Different influences were being exerted on the two sexes, apparently. What were they? By 1900, men were already marrying at a comparatively late age, and were, perhaps, little affected by the factors thought to favour later marriage, but for young women, schooling was far commoner by 1931 – at ages 15–19, 23 per cent of girls were literate in 1911 and as many as 52 per cent in 1931 – and they were affected by the changing sex ratio in the total population. In relation to the number of females, there were 5 per cent fewer men in 1931 than

TABLE 11: MARITAL STATUS OF PERSONS AGED 15 AND OVER, 1901–73 (PERCENTAGES)

Census of	Single	Married	Widowed	Divorced
Male				
1901	36	59	5	—
1931	37	58	5	—
1946	34	62	4	—
1960	28	69	3	—
1973*	32	65	2	1
Female				
1901	25	60	15	—
1931	29	56	14	1
1946	26	61	12	1
1960	23	65	11	1
1973*	27	63	9	1

* Non-Turkish-Cypriot population

in 1911; consequently girls' prospects of marriage were diminishing, or at least being postponed.

In contrast to the consistent pattern up to 1931, unexpected changes were taking place by 1946, as both men and women began to marry at younger ages again – despite yet further improvements in education and a continued fall in the masculinity ratio. The trend is shown clearly in Table 12, which gives the percentages of persons in the younger adult ages who had never married, beginning in 1901. Over the age of 35 no differential between 1901 and 1931 was found, and as the 5 per cent enumerated as unmarried may well have included a few widowed and divorced persons in error, the proportion of genuinely single people over 45 was probably as low as it could possibly be; it was particularly in the group 20–24 that a new pattern was emerging.

A down-swing in the proportions single from 1931 to 1960 is obvious, followed by a rapid rise to roughly earlier levels. With 83 per cent unmarried in the 20–24 group, the males are now back at their 1901 proportion – but hardly because of rural poverty and

TABLE12: PERCENTAGES OF SINGLE PERSONS
IN SELECTED AGE GROUPS, 1901–73

	20–24	25–29	30–34
Male			
1901	82	33	
1931	83	33	
1946	74	40	18
1960	64	26	10
1973*	82	35	8
1946 Greek Orthodox	76	41	18
Moslem	64	31	16
Female			
1901	45	11	
1931	57	18	
1946	52	26	13
1960	44	18	10
1973*	61	26	10
1946 Greek Orthodox	58	29	15
Moslem	27	10	4

* Non-Turkish-Cypriot population

indebtedness today; and there is a higher proportion of single females now than has ever been recorded before. By 30–34 years, however, it is likely that more Cypriots are married now than ever before – owing in part, perhaps, to the elimination of certain diseases which previously rendered marriage impracticable for some people. Recent changes in the pattern have, then, not been consistent in different age groups, and have been less marked in the case of females than of males.

In both Tables 11 and 12, 1960 stands out as an exceptional year. That marriage took place earlier up to 1960 when educational standards were rising fast may seem surprising, since longer schooling is generally considered a factor in postponing marriage. But whether this theory was valid for Cyprus is not clear, as Percival concluded in 1946 that except for girls going on to post-secondary education, the time spent at school did not greatly affect the age at marriage. Probably a clearer reason for supposing that the incidence of marriage should have decreased was the rapidly growing urban population – 19 per cent of the total in 1931, but 36 per cent in 1960. And again, it might be thought that the acute civil disturbances of the late 1950s could have led to some postponement of marriage. However, other reasons tending in the opposite direction can also be seen. As the deficit of males in the population increased after 1931, girls probably tended to marry earlier. The latter point was noted by Percival: some 700 more girls than men were reaching the average age of marriage every year, he calculated, and once the existing pool of men over that age became unavailable for marriage for any reason, it would be open to girls to find husbands below it – signifying that the men must marry younger or the women remain unmarried. Another cause was also seen by Percival – 'generally easier circumstances'; he was able to identify unusually high marriage rates in certain years which he designated as 'fairly prosperous'. In populations which have been deprived of adequate schooling by poverty and have customarily married young – as in many developing countries – increasing affluence enables education to be lengthened, and as a consequence marriage tends to be postponed. In Cyprus, however, marriage already took place at a comparatively late age, so when growing prosperity enabled parents' obligations to their children regarding property to be fulfilled earlier, it was natural that the age of marriage should fall. We may speculate about another reason too. In the 1950s emigration was on an unprecedented scale. Did the prospect of moving to another country tend to advance marriages? In Cyprus it probably did, because the flow was not of young men to unknown lands, but rather of family groups to countries well known to them; young people might, then, have preferred early marriage to waiting and travelling at different times. The later marriages after 1960 seen in Table 12 must be due in part to the exclusion of the Turkish-Cypriots from the 1973 figures.

Widowhood has been decreasing as the expectation of life has risen. The point is seen clearly in the proportions of widowed persons aged 45 and over – 39 per cent in 1931 but only 22 per cent in 1973. No doubt the proportion will decrease further, as the young and middle-aged people now enjoying longer expectancies become elderly in the future.

Divorces have always been few – between 110 and 160 annually in the Greek-Cypriot population in the last few years and slightly more among the Turkish-Cypriots, signifying a divorce *rate* some four times higher in the latter group. Nevertheless, the government's *Demographic Report* gives nearly as much space to comment on divorce as on marriage, pointing out that the average duration of marriage before divorce is about seven years, and that usually the couple has a child or children under 15. In 1978 divorces secured on petition by the husband outnumbered those by the wife by about two to one, and among the former, 'persistent refusal to return to the conjugal home in spite of invitation by the bishop' was the commonest ground, while most wives petitioned on account of 'malicious desertion for a period exceeding three years'. 'Though worded in a different way these grounds are very similar and can be simply considered as abandonment or desertion', the *Demographic Report* observes, adding that the formal grounds for divorce should be distinguished from the true grounds of family disruption. Perhaps it would not be surprising if the latter included the events of the last fifteen years such as civil disturbance, war, and emigration.

The average age at marriage calculated by Hajnal's method – which, referring to the lifetime experience of persons aged 15 to 50, is not coincident with the current average age at marriage such as given in the *Demographic Report* – helps to illustrate the changing trends of marriage.

	Male	Female
1901	27·1	22·3
1931	27·4	24·0
1946	26·5	24·0
1960	24·6	22·6
1973*	26·3	24·1

* Excluding Turkish-Cypriots

There was never any tradition of permanent celibacy to

account for comparatively late marriage. 'In the village all children of both sexes, if not seriously deformed or handicapped, must marry and do marry . . . It is also considered proper to marry them off as young as legally possible, and to have no unmarried daughters over 25 or unmarried sons over 30.'[1] In the towns the age for marrying was higher, but eventual celibacy just as rare. A primary cause of late marriage must have been the passing on of property to children at the time of their marriage instead of on the death of the parents – the dowry system. It was traditionally thought that the new family should have a separate home and domestic economy immediately on marriage, and usually the bride brought a house to the marriage, although in some villages this was the prerogative of the bridegroom; and the house remained in the possession of the partner who provided it. To the house was added whatever land and animals could be made available. The bridegroom, for his part, was expected to contribute furniture, linen, and land or money if possible. Equipping the children for marriage was, then, a major task in the lives of parents – perhaps the most exacting duty of all. The demands it made were such that the family tended to focus its efforts on one child at a time; to concentrate on the second after the first was married off; and so on. It was not unnatural, then, that engagements were long – up to four years. Because the dowry was an important aid during early married life, young people without one, particularly young women, were liable to have difficulty in finding a suitable partner.

Linked to the customs of marriage was the system of inheriting land – the most precious commodity in Cyprus after water – to the extent that urbanised Cypriots still set great store by the possession of a plot, even though they hardly ever see it. There was a strong feeling in favour of keeping villagers' land within the village community whenever possible, and it was not irrelevant that Loizos found in the village which he investigated in the 1960s that some four marriages out of five were between persons born there. Most villagers had some land, he observed, and since those who did not were able to find work nearby, most were able to marry within the village, in accordance with the traditional desire that land, wealth, and marriage partners be kept within the control of the village. In consequence, many villagers were inter-related, which in turn strengthened the village community.

It is difficult to doubt that the dowry system influenced both the age at marriage and parents' ideas of family size and of the spacing of children. Another consequence, probably, was shown earlier – extremely low proportions of divorced persons. In the case of the Greeks at least, such figures were not due to prompt re-marriage after divorce, for, as *Lysi* observes, a divorced female could only look forward to the severely restricted social life of an unmarried girl. For a Greek, divorce was sanctioned by canon law, but was so rare that at the 1921 census, for instance, no more than thirty males and a hundred females declared themselves as divorced; it was against all training and instinct. Making the marriage permanent was often important to each family, because its economic viability was linked to the new partnership. Long engagements gave the couple and their families ample opportunity of assessing the chance of a successful partnership. The couple therefore found themselves in a world where family bonds were strong, and there was an imbued reluctance to endanger them. A fourth demographic consequence of the dowry system must have been the migration of young men from their homes to those of their brides. The movement cannot be traced in the censuses, since departures from a particular area would be compensated by the inflow of other young men to marry local girls. Certainly many men married girls from their own village, so it was not always that they moved away, but such migrations must have occurred to an extent which would have been unusual in most countries.

In recent years, changes have occurred in the old concepts of marriage and dowry. The principle of inheritance at the time of marriage continues to be maintained in the Greek community, but the form of the dowry is changing. Since the 1974 war, many parents have held no land to pass on except in the form of promises to be fulfilled after the inter-communal dispute is settled, so providing a son with the best possible education is tending to replace the gift of land. But while land is less of an economic necessity at the beginning of working life, as paid jobs proliferate, a house remains essential. So because ownership of a house, or a large contribution to its acquisition, is a great asset to a daughter in competitive bidding for a husband with good job prospects, there has been an increasing tendency for property to be inherited through daughters, an observer has pointed out. The daughter's dowry, then, has not changed, although it may now be thought ideal to provide girls with a good education as well as a home. A new characteristic is said to be the weakening of the endogamous nature of marriage, partly because the people of a village which was displaced in 1974 did not always end up in the same place, and partly because compulsory military service, introduced in the same year, removed young men from their home towns and villages for two years at a susceptible time of their lives. For young people to live together in trial marriages is another practice which has increased in recent years. Whatever the future circumstances, some of these innovations will remain, we may think, because such trends, once ingrained, do not change easily.

Distribution, urbanisation and internal migration

The six administrative districts differ widely in size – Nicosia, for instance, is over four times as large as Kyrenia – and consequently the totals of their populations vary greatly too, but in the early years of British rule, the *densities* of population in the districts were remarkably similar, as Table 13 shows.

Similar densities in the districts suggest similar geographic and economic characteristics; yet within the island there is a variety of plain and mountain, wheat land and forest, scrub and intensive cultivation. Was it the case that most, or all, districts shared these characteristics? Five of them contained mountainous areas, the exception being Larnaca; in the Troodos range indeed, district boundaries were found at some of the highest points, for in a pattern centuries old the administrative area stretched outwards from the district town until it reached roughly the highest point, and there the next district took over. It was this element of isolation which enabled a Governor to say as late as 1939 that the districts varied considerably in the occupations and outlook of their inhabitants, and that each had a strong spirit of local independence and rivalry.[2] While the peaks and high forests of the Troodos mountains were virtually uninhabited, there was still considerable habitation at quite high altitudes, because of the crops to be grown there – vines and various fruits and vegetables, all of which required the labour of many people in a small area. Nicosia district included both the Mesaoria plain and mountains

TABLE 13: POPULATION GROWTH AND DENSITY IN THE DISTRICTS 1881–1960

| | Percentage growth | | | Persons per sq. mile | |
	1881–31	1931–46	1946–60*	1881	1960
Nicosia	95	33	36	54	194
Kyrenia	71	24	8	48	125
Famagusta	87	32	17	41	150
Larnaca	103	24	9	61	136
Limassol	98	30	32	53	200
Paphos	54	23	8	49	108
CYPRUS	87	29	23	50	161

*Excluding British and others in 1960, the only census year when comparatively large numbers of British service men and families were enumerated as part of the total population

to the north and the south-west; Limassol district included a wide coastal belt, a large area of foothills, and the southern side of Troodos; Famagusta shared the Mesaoria and the Kyrenia range with Nicosia. That Larnaca, almost without mountains, had the lowest rural density in 1881 seems surprising; it was probably due to the poverty of its agricultural land and scarcity of water.

Comparisons between the population densities of different countries can be misleading because of factors which they leave unrevealed – how much of the land is non-arable or uninhabitable, for instance. For what they may be worth, some comparative densities are given here.

	Persons per square mile
Cyprus (1931)	97
Crete (1920)	109
Greece (1920)	98
Malta (1931)	2,016
Sardinia (1931)	104
Sicily (1931)	391
Turkey (1927)	47

Clearly Cyprus had a number of those characteristics which determine population density in common with Crete, Greece, and Sardinia, fewer with Turkey and Sicily, and very few indeed with Malta. Since emigration of Cypriots in the working ages occurred consistently after 1901, it seems that at a density of around seventy persons per square mile overall, or about fifty-five per square mile of rural area, agriculture in Cyprus at least could not quite support the population at the rather low standard of living obtaining before the Second World War.

Urbanisation was an important factor in the differential growth in districts. To begin with, it proceeded slowly, the six district towns containing 17 per cent of the population at the time of the first census and no more than 19 per cent fifty years later. Such a pace seems surprising at a time when the towns of many countries were developing by leaps and bounds, but it may be explained by several factors having particular effect in Cyprus. Firstly, the island's tiny industry hardly expanded, for reasons such as lack of capital, a small home market, and lack of raw materials. Secondly, the 'push' factor, the inability of the countryside to provide a living, was limited in extent, because population growth was only moderate and agricultural methods were improving. Thirdly, both the miniature scale of the country and Cypriot custom ran contrary to forced migrations to the towns. It was possible for some people to stay in their rural habitat while doing urban work; and intense family loyalties led to supporting the indigent at home rather than sending them off to inhospitable towns. The inhabitants of the towns were, then, fewer than those making regular use of them, and consequently the towns never became a refuge for a workless rural population. Fourthly, the outlet of emigration, which affected nearly every village, helped to slow down urban growth. It was a characteristic not peculiar to either Cyprus or the period, for recent studies by the Council of Europe show that large proportions of mainland Greek and Turkish workers in Europe come from the villages of their home countries. A fifth reason was the changing balance of Greeks and Turks in the population. The latter were the more urbanised, 26 per cent of them living in the towns in 1881, but only 13 per cent of the Greeks. During the next fifty years the proportion of Turks in the population fell: had they maintained their 1 : 3 ratio, the towns would have grown faster because of the greater Turkish presence there.

The amounts by which the urban and rural areas and the six towns industrially expanded varied considerably, as Table 14 shows. Exceptional growth up to 1931 is seen in Larnaca and Famagusta towns. The former expanded slowly, after a concentration of population there under the Turks. It had been the residence of the consular corps, the centre of commerce, and the home of the Roman Catholics, the 'Latins', who virtually monopolised trade. The town's population numbered some 15,000 in the 1850s, it was reported – almost the size of Nicosia – but on the arrival of the British, it became a normal district town, and twenty years later had only 8,000 inhabitants. Famagusta grew fast, for a quite different reason: it had been almost abandoned by the Turks. 'It is now inhabited by a miserable population of 500 Turks,' a British consular agent wrote in 1843, while another mentioned 300 inhabitants and spoke of an insalubrious heap of ruins. Christians were not allowed in the town; they lived in nearby Varosha. After finding Famagusta a mere shadow of its former self, the British put the harbour into working order and constructed a railway to Nicosia, and, by the 1911 census, it was again a town of importance. Paphos town

TABLE 14: URBAN AND RURAL GROWTH IN THE DISTRICTS, 1881–1960

| | Percentage growth | | | | Percentage urban | |
| | 1881–1931 | | 1931–60 | | 1931 | 1960 |
	Urban	Rural	Urban	Rural		
Nicosia	105	93	184	26	30	47
Kyrenia	79	71	61	34	9	11
Famagusta	250	75	287	27	13	30
Larnaca	52	135	67	28	28	34
Limassol	150	84	184	50	27	41
Paphos	105	50	101	25	10	16
CYPRUS	112	82	170	31	19	36

expanded by somewhat more than the national average in the first fifty years, but as a result, clearly, of some migration from the rural part of the district, due, in its turn, to the use of the town as a staging point for people migrating to other districts or countries overseas. One of those districts was Limassol, where the town was the centre of the export trade in wine and carobs. The census reports made unfortunately few comments on any subject, but the Superintendent of the first census was alive to unusual movement in Limassol district, observing that there were more males than females because of in-migration due to the demand for labour at the port and in the numerous vineyards. Two years earlier, Baker had observed that 'the port of Limassol will eventually become the chief commercial centre of Cyprus', adding that in the twelve months since the British occupation, there had been a decided rise in the value of town property and that the annual municipal receipts had increased by seven times. Movement into some of the towns at least was, then, evident within three years of the arrival of the British. Nicosia town, however, may have resembled Larnaca in losing population after 1878, for British reports gave its total as about 16,000, *mostly Mohammedans*, at some time before that date, whereas the 1881 census found less than 15,000 in the town and some of the surrounding villages. Whatever loss there may have been was quickly restored.

Beginning in the 1930s a much greater shift of population to the towns occurred – on the scale of some 100,000 persons in thirty years, we may deduce. By 1960, not only was 36 per cent a large proportion of the population to be found in the towns of a non-industrialised country, but even more people were commuting to them – a point attracting the comment by Attalides that a large proportion of Nicosia's working class lived outside, and that the lack of physical deterioration and visible housing problems within the town was due to the fact that such matters were concealed within the nearby villages. In the absence of large industrial expansion, it was the urban opportunities for non-industrial work, in addition to lessening demand for labour on the land, which brought about the flow of population to the towns. Among the six, only Kyrenia and Paphos remained purely district centres; three of the others were ports, and the fourth, Nicosia, was the administrative capital, so these four expanded according to the needs of the whole island. Alongside Famagusta, where the Venetian walls and the sea imposed strict limits on growth, the new town of Varosha was becoming an important seaside resort, graced by perfect sands – and marred, some may think, by a rash of utilitarian hotels.

The rapid growth of the towns was by no means even over the thirty years. It can be estimated that natural increase there from 1931 to 1946 amounted to some 22,000 persons and was supplemented by in-migration of about 17,000 more. Then came a striking contrast: between 1946 and 1960 the town populations increased by 80 per cent and the remainder by a mere 10 per cent, the former figure representing some 31,000 persons by natural increase, while the addition through migration was as much as 59,000. This was a sign, surely, of radical changes in economic and social conditions. Certainly the rural population continued to grow, but by a mere 33,000 persons; and since daily commuting from the villages was becoming commonplace, one must wonder whether the workers in the countryside increased at all. This point will be examined in Chapter 7.

Unlike the villages, five of the towns are on the sea. This does not signify that the Cypriots are a seafaring people in the way that, say, the British or the Malays are said to be; the contrary is actually the case. The sites of the towns came about for historical reasons – the island had to be outward-looking, both in the commerce of goods and the traffic of people; under the Lusignans, it was a port, Famagusta, which became the showplace of the Mediterranean, and other regimes too needed points of entry and exit. There were several ports rather than one central one, for two reasons: internal communications were tedious and costly – and sometimes dangerous – until the British built roads; and, secondly, there was a need for internal trade because different crops were produced in different places – wheat on the Mesaoria plain and wine near Limassol, for instance. The ports were, then, sited to serve their hinterlands: Famagusta was the closest to the Mesaoria and the fertile Karpass peninsula; Larnaca was easily accessible to Nicosia; Limassol, sheltered from the prevailing west wind, served the wine and carob country; Paphos was long-established, having been the port for the temple of Aphrodite in classical times and later the Roman administrative centre where that prudent governor Sergius Paulus was converted to

Christianity by St Paul. The traditional use of all the ports continued into the British period, despite the coming of roads; for instance, the mail contract up to 1914 required the vessel carrying the mail to Egypt (to connect with western Europe) to call not merely at one port but at all four.

Turks shared with Greeks in both the urban life and the movement to the towns, but to a lessening degree as time passed. Their presence in the towns was still a little greater than in the total population in 1960 – 20 and 18 per cent respectively – but it had fallen consistently since 1881. It was apparently a Turkish characteristic to live in either the town centres or the smaller villages – one extreme or the other. Detail from Nicosia in 1960 illustrates the point: Turks comprised 20 per cent of the district population, but 32 per cent in the town, 17 in the rural areas – and only 15 in the suburbs. In the larger villages – those with over 2,000 persons – less than a tenth of the inhabitants were Turks. This predilection was accentuated by the disturbances of the 1950s, which caused many Turkish-Cypriots to leave their villages and seek safety in the larger Turkish communities.[3]

Little contemporary comment about rural-to-urban migration seems to have been made, although Percival did not overlook the point. By examining unpublished sex ratios, he traced six groups of 'emigration villages' – areas where, in the working ages, women outnumbered men by not less than five to four, and where, he presumed, migration 'either overseas or into the army or the towns' was enough to upset social conditions. The areas were: Klirou to Pelekhori, in Nicosia district; the western hillside villages, in Kyrenia district; Yialousa and the villages along the coast, together with the northern Mesaoria, in Famagusta district; and the Dhrousha-Stroumbi area in Paphos district. Using other unpublished data, he noted that two-thirds of the migrants went to the local town, but few to villages in other districts. In general, then, a village was inhabited by persons born either within it or in neighbouring villages.

Percival's use here of sex ratios leads us to suppose that males heavily outnumbered females in the towns at the time. This was not actually the case, the ratios there being: 1931 – 1,022 males per 1,000 females; 1946 – 1,031; 1960 – 991. It appears, then, that his six areas were never typical of all rural areas, and in some of the six at least, the shortage of males in 1946 was not permanent either, there being in 1973 not under 800 males per 1,000 females in the Lefkara and Dhrousha areas, but 930 and 906 respectively. In 1946, we may recollect, emigrants probably still comprised more males than females, and enlistments in the armed forces and auxiliary services certainly did, so exceptional deficiencies of males could easily have occurred in particular places.

As the censuses listed the towns and villages separately, the published tables included totals for (a) the six towns together and (b) all the villages together. Although these divisions were not referred to as 'urban' and 'rural' before 1960, they appear to have been so regarded, and certainly no better definition of the terms was suggested. In modern usage, 'urban' pertains to a locality with more than a certain number of inhabitants – 2,000 to 40,000, perhaps, according to the country concerned – rather than to a town which happens to be an administrative centre, and it is suggested that in Cyprus 2,000 might be a reasonable dividing line. It is an arbitrary choice and 3,000 might do as well, but on looking at the Cyprus countryside, one may imagine that ordinary people's lives took on a rather different shape once a group of around 2,000 was formed, usually with its church, shop, coffee house, and two or three tradesmen, not to speak of an all-weather road and a local bus or lorry. Hereafter, then, agglomerations of 2,000 and more persons are considered urban, as well as Kyrenia town, which, although an administrative centre, had a population of less than 2,000 up to 1931.

In 1881 there were two villages of over 2,000 persons – Lapithos (2,370) and Morphou (2,267) – and the urban population comprised 19 per cent of the total, whereas the six towns alone contained 17 per cent. In 1931, however, there were eleven such villages (and six more with totals of only just under 2,000) and the urban population now comprised 28 per cent of the total – a considerable proportion for an almost completely non-industrialised country. And in addition, numbers of Cypriots led existences which were both urban and rural, having jobs in the town but living in a village. Strong influences existed to hold villagers to their villages, even if they worked outside them. Distances were small, and particularly after the advent of the motor bus, travelling into town to work was often less exacting than the journey today's commuters put up with in many western cities. Because of the fragmentation of immovable property, very many people had a direct stake in the land. Property values were rising in the towns, so the house to be given to the daughter on marriage was more easily built – and for many people, could only be built – in a village. The village had been a living community for much longer than anyone could remember, and keeping it together and maintaining its strength was a tradition and a principle almost as strong as upholding the honour of the family. For such reasons, many people continued to live as villagers while spending a large part of their lives in the towns – the best of both worlds, many people in the developed countries might think today – the towns were smaller than they might have been, and to read that only 28 per cent of the population were urban is almost misleading. In 1960 that percentage was 48.

As Table 13 shows growth in Larnaca district of 103 per cent in fifty years and in Paphos of 54 per cent while the total population increased by 87 per cent, it is clear that some people moved into Larnaca and some away from Paphos – but not necessarily the same people. Unfortunately, detail of the process is not available, since while the censuses asked a question on the place of birth, they tabulated the answers by country only, except in 1946 and 1973. From the 1931 census, for instance, we know that two persons enumerated in Nicosia were born in the Falkland Islands, but not how many were born in Larnaca and the other districts. Therefore the best measure of inter-district migration is usually the excess or deficit in a district at a particular census when the enumerated population is compared with the population expected on the basis of the country's inter-censal growth; within its limits it provides a fair indication, for instance in the figures for Nicosia district (shown opposite).

Here we see that between 1881 and 1921 there was net movement in both directions which almost cancelled out, but that thereafter in-migration was of a different order. In 1960, some 10 per cent of Nicosia's population must have moved into the district during the previous fourteen years.

In making such comparisons for different decades and districts, percentages are more informative than absolute numbers. They can be calculated not only for each district in each decade, but for the district town and rural areas and the Greek Orthodox and the Moslems within districts as well, with Table 15 resulting for

	Population	Excess/Deficit
1881	56,312	
1891	61,695	− 1,600
1901	71.289	+ 1,389
1911	81,497	− 913
1921	93,765	+ 1,347
1931	110,010	+ 4,993
1946	145,965	+ 3,700
1960	204,282	+18,300

Nicosia district, to give one example. The see-saw movement in the first four decades seen earlier is reflected in the column 'Population', but we observe that the oscillations were largely those of the urban population, while the rural population was less affected by migration. Possibly a class of urban labourer was developing, moving from town to town as work offered. Because the urban–rural growth pattern in Nicosia is blurred by the rapid expansion of the suburbs – those nearby villages which took on an urban type of growth and finally joined up physically with the walled city which was itself incapable of outward expansion – what an observer might have regarded as urban growth was actually more marked than is suggested by Table 15. Greek Orthodox and Moslem movement also differed, with Moslems

TABLE 15: NICOSIA DISTRICT: NET MIGRATION OF POPULATION, URBAN AND RURAL, GREEK ORTHODOX AND MOSLEM, IN INTER-CENSAL PERIODS, 1881–1931 (PERCENTAGES OF ACTUAL POPULATION)

	Population	Urban	Rural	Greek Orthodox	Moslem
1881–91	−2·6	− 3·6	−2·3	−5·2	+3·4
1891–01	+1·9	+ 3·9	+1·4	+0·8	+4·7
1901–11	−1·1	− 6·2	+0·1	+0·8	−2·4
1911–21	+1·4	+ 2·0	+1·3	+0·8	+3·4
1921–31	+4·5	+12·1	+3·0	+3·0	+7·5

migrating into the district fairly consistently in modest numbers, while there was coming and going of Greeks in numbers which were smaller until 1921.

Lack of space precludes the reproduction of Table 15 for all the districts, but a similar summary for each district over the fifty-year period is given in Table 16. Here, three points are outstanding. The move out of Paphos district was large and consistent; it amounted to 8 per cent in the 1920s alone; and it was shared by Greeks and Turks alike. Secondly, a loss also occurred in Kyrenia district, probably for the same reason as in Paphos – isolation. Much of Kyrenia's coastal plain lies within a few miles of Nicosia, but was as effectively separated from the capital by mountains as Paphos was by 100 miles of partly made road. Thirdly, the proportion of Moslem movement was greater than that of the Greeks. It was not a coincidence that Paphos had in 1881 by far the largest proportion of Moslems of any district and lost more of its population than any other district. The direction of the Moslem movement did not coincide with that of the Greeks, focusing on Nicosia and Larnaca, not only over the fifty years but in every separate decade.

In two of the three subsequent inter-censal periods a different measure became available, as the 1946 and 1973 counts tabulated district of birth. Lifetime migration was thus shown – Mr X, for example, was enumerated in Nicosia district but reported that

TABLE 16: ALL DISTRICTS: NET MIGRATION OF
POPULATION, URBAN AND RURAL, GREEK ORTHODOX
AND MOSLEM, 1881–1931
(PERCENTAGES OF POPULATION IN 1931)

	Population	Urban	Rural	Greek Orthodox	Moslem
Nicosia	+ 4·3	+ 8·9	+ 3·6	− 1·1	+16·1
Kyrenia	− 9·0	+ 4·2	− 9·5	− 8·5	−21·1
Famagusta	+ 0·1	+ 4·7	− 6·6	+ 1·5	− 6·3
Larnaca	+ 8·0	− 2·3	+20·3	+ 7·9	+16·6
Limassol	+ 5·5	+25·3	− 1·7	+ 8·7	−10·0
Paphos	−21·4	+ 8·8	−24·8	−15·5	−22·8

he had been born in Larnaca district – in contradistinction to the migration since the previous census discussed above. The census question fails to trace multiple moves or a move away from and a subsequent return to one's native district, and to record moves by people who have died; and, further, the accuracy of tables of birthplace is always open to some doubt, for it depends on, firstly, the detail required by the question, and secondly, not only the respondent's memory but sometimes his knowledge of geography as well. The 1946 question read, 'If you were born in Cyprus, name the village and the district.' In larger countries, the enumerator may not be familiar with the name of the village given to him, or the migrant himself with the name of the administrative district. When uncertainties arise, the district of enumeration tends to be entered as that of birth as well, so migration is understated. Cypriots, however, were probably aware of their exact birthplace.

Net lifetime migration thus estimated and net inter-censal migration calculated by means of district projections are shown in Table 17. Despite the inherent weaknesses in the data, it is clear that Nicosia and Limassol districts gained population before 1946, and that Kyrenia, Larnaca, and, more particularly, Paphos lost. But the scale of inter-district migration was apparently quite

TABLE 17: LIFETIME AND ESTIMATED INTER-CENSAL MIGRATION BETWEEN DISTRICTS, 1946 AND 1973

District	1946		1973*	
	Lifetime migration	Migration 1931–46	Lifetime migration	Migration 1960–73
Nicosia	+11,000	+3,700	+21,300	+12,700
Kyrenia	− 3,400	−1,200	− 6,600	− 1,500
Famagusta	− 1,300	+2,000	− 1,100	− 200
Larnaca	− 200	−2,400	− 2,100	− 4,200
Limassol	+ 2,100	+ 600	+ 2,800	− 1,100
Paphos	− 8,200	−2,700	−14,300	− 5,700

* Non-Turkish-Cypriot population

small, and indeed other 1946 data show that it was exceeded by lifetime rural-to-urban migration – confirming Percival's observation that most moves out of a village were to the local town. In the 1960s the direction of migration was simplifying even more: it was concentrated on Nicosia. But the pace was slackening; Nicosia took in only 12,700 persons in twelve and a half years – no more than 7 per cent of its population – after an estimated 18,300 in the previous inter-censal period. Perhaps the pattern of life and work which changed radically after 1945 was settling down again. At the same time, declining population growth was helping to reduce pressure to leave the countryside – or alternatively the property boom in the towns compelled more and more would-be migrants to keep their village homes and commute. As for the urban population, growth amounted to a mere 27 per cent; yet even so the rural population decreased. This decrease marked a watershed in Cyprus' history, we may think, and although in 1973 the rural population still outnumbered the urban population by about three to two, a time when country-dwellers would be in a minority was in sight for the first time.[4]

It is interesting to observe what is almost certainly understatement of migration as derived from the 1973 census. Two examples follow. Nicosia recorded lifetime in-migration of 11,000 in 1946, followed by estimated in-migration of 31,000 in the next two inter-censal periods, but lifetime in-migration of only 21,300 in 1973; and Paphos recorded lifetime out-migration of 8,200 in 1946, followed by estimated out-migration of 16,200 in the next two inter-censal periods, but lifetime out-migration of only 14,300 in 1973. Although the equations (11,000+31,000=21,300 in the case of Nicosia) cannot be expected to balance because of deaths and multiple migrations during the period, the discrepancy seems over-large, implying that many people reported incorrectly that they had been born in the district where they were enumerated. This conclusion is supported by the smaller proportions of locally-born found by Attalides' survey of Nicosia in the early 1970s.

Between 1963 and 1974 migration was influenced by a new factor – the need for physical security. It caused Turkish-Cypriots to leave their smaller, or more isolated, settlements for the bigger ones, on a scale which was reportedly large in relation to the community's size. By an estimate of Attalides, some 15,000

Turkish-Cypriots – nearly 15 per cent of the community – moved into Nicosia alone after the conflicts of 1963–4,[5] and according to another report 1,500 left their villages in Paphos district – about one in six of the total in the area.[6] By 1970, 20,000 Turkish-Cypriots were registered as refugees with their author-ities. Altogether a substantial number of villages were evacuated by the Turkish-Cypriots; on the other hand there appear to have been no reports of enforced movement on the part of Greek-Cypriots.

The 1974 war brought about a wholesale redistribution of population, culminating in the absence of Turkish-Cypriots today from the area south of the new 'Green Line', while only a very few Greek-Cypriots continue to live north of it. How the Turkish-Cypriot people are distributed in districts is not known.[7] Equivalent detail for the Greek-Cypriots, obtained from the 1976 count, is contained in Table 18. Immediately following July 1974,

TABLE 18: NON-TURKISH-CYPRIOT
POPULATION IN DISTRICTS, 1973
AND 1976

District	1973	1976
Nicosia	188,000	189,000
Kyrenia	27,000	–
Famagusta	102,000	23,000
Larnaca	45,000	79,000
Limassol	99,000	141,000
Paphos	41,000	47,000
CYPRUS	502,000	479,000

the location of the displaced Greek-Cypriots was determined by considerations such as where accommodation happened to be available, where it was practicable to construct refugee camps, where work could be found or created. Consequently the settlement pattern of late 1974 probably changed considerably before the census of 1976, and has changed again between that census and today. Further, it will alter again radically with a political settlement between the two communities. For the time being it is political, not economic and social, considerations which have largely taken charge of the population's distribution and migratory movements.

7

ECONOMIC ACTIVITY

Numbers of workers

A CENSUS question to ascertain how many people were economically active[1] was first asked in 1946, but earlier censuses obtained the same kind of information by enquiring about every individual's occupation, with an accompanying instruction to enumerators such as: 'The precise nature of occupation to be stated. A person following several distinct occupations must state each of them in order of their importance, and a landowner should be so described in addition to ordinary occupation. The occupations, if any, of women and children are to be cited, as well as those of men. Children attending school must be returned under the head of "Scholars".' (1901) Thus, everyone had an entry, and the decision on who was economically active was made in the central office, not by the enumerator. However, in that particular year, many landowners were apparently entered twice, once as a landowner, once as a farmer or as having some other occupation. Here, concepts were confused: enquiring about land ownership was a legitimate census question, but owning land was no more an occupation then for census purposes than owning a motor car is today. By 1931 the census was distinguishing between workers aged under and over 15 and persons with and without occupation – identifying the economically active in modern terms, in fact. A very comprehensive enquiry was made in 1946. Not one but six questions were asked:

Economic category (e.g. having an occupation, house-worker, unemployed)
Is the main occupation agricultural or non-agricultural?
Secondary occupation
For non-agricultural occupations
  – occupation
  – industry
  – status (employer, employed, etc.),

137

in addition to a separate question about the ownership of land or livestock. Satisfactory results were obtained, except, possibly, in respect of the time reference period, which seemed at one point to be the present and at another the 'last twelve months', while at a third future employment was mentioned. The 1960 census, on the other hand, was precise on the point, the first question on economic activity reading: 'Did this person work at any time during the week started 17th October and ended on 22nd October 1960?' The phrase 'at any time' was reinforced by another, which emphasised that work for only one hour qualified. This was a new idea, and it seems unfortunate that its results had to differ markedly from those obtained both earlier and in 1973. Other questions about occupation, industry, employment status, and some matters which were not eventually tabulated such as the means of getting to work, combined with four questions on income and another on the number of pieces of land owned in separate villages, constituted a formidable enquiry. Altogether, concepts, definitions, and questions have differed very considerably since 1891, and the difficulty of reconciling the results is not helped by the absence of explanation in the census reports except in 1946. Some adjustments, and even guesses, have, then, been needed to compare data from different years.

What proportions of the population were reported to be economically active? The Superintendent in 1891 observed that there was particular difficulty in getting an accurate return of occupations, and that the reported activity rates probably did not mean much – 72 per cent of males between 25 and 45 years of age, for instance. Another rate, 67 per cent of males aged 20–24, was much too low for an agricultural society in which post-primary education hardly existed. Under-employment was no doubt common in the rural areas in the slack seasons, but *un*employment on that scale seems inconceivable. In the 1901 census, a different problem arose – the double counting of landowners already mentioned: if they were included, the percentages active rose to over 100. No doubt many landowners were actually farmers and were correctly reported as such, while others were absentee owners and did different work in the village or town. In the next three census reports, a different problem was created by the omission of the earlier cross-tabulations of occupation by age. Although in many countries there are young children who do work such as minding goats and helping with the harvest, it is usual to ignore the population under a certain age when considering economic activity; 15 is often taken as a dividing line. So in 1911, for instance, it is only after omitting 'children' and those having no occupation and making other adjustments that matching the remainder with the population aged 15 and over shows 79 per cent of males aged 15 and over to have been working. Since the equivalent figures in 1946 and 1960, when far more young men were in school, were 88 to 90 per cent, 79 was also an unreasonably low figure. The true situation up to about 1940 must rather have been that most males, from around 10 years of age until their deaths, did what work was necessary, in the light of their strength and fitness and of the seasonal needs of their farms or the farms on which they worked; under-employment was rife, so casual work elsewhere was often sought, but unemployment, that is being without a job of any kind over a signficant period, was hardly known.

The proportions economically active from 1946 onwards are shown in Table 19. In 1960 the proportions resulting from including persons working for only one hour in a week were likely to be high, and in fact were, but a point of interest is seen on comparing the 1946 and 1973 figures: overall the percentage of

TABLE 19: PERCENTAGES OF THE POPULATION AGED 15 AND OVER ECONOMICALLY ACTIVE, 1946–73

| | 1946 | | 1960 | | 1973* | |
Age	Male	Female	Male	Female	Male	Female
15–24†	76	25	78	42	41	31
25–54	97	20	99	44	97	26
55 and over	77	13	84	31	57	10
15 and over†	86	20	90	41	71	23
15–19†	63	25	?	?	21	22
20–24	92	27	?	?	66	41

* Non-Turkish-Cypriot population only
† In 1946, for 15 read 14
(These age groups are those used in the 1960 census tables)

men working fell by the latter date, while that of working women rose. Here we may detect three separate influences on working habits. The first was that very obvious feature in Cypriot life, the expansion of secondary and post-secondary education; because of it, few males under 20 were free to take jobs by 1973, and fewer aged 20–24 than previously. Secondly, because the urban population had grown proportionately, more elderly men were losing the opportunity to help out on the farm for as long as their strength lasted; at the same time, retirement, compulsory at a certain age for many employees, became a recognised concept for the first time. Thirdly, women were taking paid employment by 1973, competing with men for clerical and other jobs. The youngest and oldest age groups were chiefly affected by such influences. Between 25 and 54, on the other hand, little variation in the proportions active occurred, because those ages were less susceptible to rising educational standards and ideas of retirement; the men continued to earn a livelihood and the women to bring up their children, as they always had.

Evidence of any influence which religion might exert on working patterns was given by only one census, that of 1946. The percentages of workers in the Greek Orthodox and Moslem populations aged 14 and over then were:

	Male	Female
Greek Orthodox	89	21
Moslem	92	18

Since it is commonly said that Islam tends to discourage women from economic activity, these figures for females may be thought questionable – and possibly they are, but for a different reason. The worth in general of such data for females will be discussed shortly.

Corresponding detail for urban and rural areas was published in 1960 and 1973, showing in the latter year that larger proportions of both men and women worked in the towns than the country. Owing to the factors of schooling and retirement just mentioned, larger proportions are normally found in the country, as they actually were in Cyprus in 1960, and it is difficult to see the reason for the exception in 1973. Possibly either the timing of

140

the census – it was taken in April, whereas the 1960 census was held in December – or something in the question or the relevant instruction caused a few rural people to report incorrectly that they were not working.

The difficulties of assessing the economic activity of Cypriot men are far exceeded by those concerning women. According to the censuses, the proportions of working females aged 15 and over have ranged from 18 to 40 per cent. It is in the work of women in particular that the uncertainties of measuring economic activity come to light, and in Cyprus two are seen clearly – what constitutes economic activity, and which time reference period is most appropriate? 'Women engaged only in household duties in their own homes are excluded from the economically active population' is the United Nations' expression of a generally accepted concept, but since in populations practising smallholding agriculture, household duties frequently include keeping chickens or growing vegetables in the back yard and helping in the fields at harvest time, distinguishing between household duties and economic activity is difficult, if not impossible.[2] Even the use of a clear time reference period does not solve the problem, as the author found in conducting censuses elsewhere: anyone who had worked for a third of normal working hours in the past year was to be considered economically active, but although rural women's work was discussed at length in the enumerators' training courses, it was found that some enumerators entered all the women as economically active, while others reported that none were: plainly they had not actually asked the question. In Cyprus before 1960 the problem must have been as great, and reflection suggests that proportions active of 20 and 30 per cent of all those aged 15 and over were really too low. Even in 1960, when it was reported that 52 per cent of rural women aged 15 and over had worked for at least one hour in a specified week, it is questionable whether anything like a true impression of women's work in the countryside was given. In the towns, the problem of measuring women's economic activity is less acute since many women there clearly 'go out to work', but it still exists in families of shopkeepers and other small business men. The scale of the problem is seen in the following percentages of women reportedly economically active in 1960 and 1973:

	1960 Urban	1960 Rural	1973 Urban	1973 Rural
15–24	29	50	34	28
25–54	22	57	29	23

The very low qualification for economic activity required in 1960 – one hour's work in a week – created a contrast in rural areas with 1973 which did not exist among males, to whom the low qualification was largely irrelevant. Further, we may doubt whether more women really worked in the towns than in the country in the latter year. Perhaps the higher urban proportion was due to easier recognition of women 'going out to work' in the towns and to the social status attached to such activity but not to farming. Altogether, Cyprus' data on female economic activity may not be very significant in themselves, and probably do not provide useful comparisons with those of other countries.

Occupations

There is difficulty in constructing a series of occupations as reported by the censuses, for three reasons. Firstly, varying concepts of economic activity inevitably mean inconsistent numbers in individual occupations. Secondly, the occupational classifications used have differed, from 170 occupations in alphabetical order in 1901 (some of them might have been omitted, for example catgut drawer and poet), to a French classification, the Bertillon system, in 1911 and 1921, a new classification of thirty-two headings in 1931, another new one in 1946 based on the 1931 United Kingdom and Cyprus censuses, and in 1960 and 1973 the International Standard Classification of Occupations. Consequently, only the broadest headings roughly resembling each other can be compared. Thirdly, it has always been known that many Cypriots had two or more occupations. When villages were still isolated, some villagers naturally acquired skills in addition to their farm work such as building and blacksmithing and practised them for profit, while others were forced by poverty to seek paid work elsewhere when they could. The 1911 census report noted the point: 'A large

142

proportion of the population whilst engaged as agriculturalists at certain times of the year do not confine themselves to this pursuit but find other means of livelihood when not working on their land, a considerable number being employed as labourers on government roads and works, whilst others find temporary employment in towns and large villages.' With greater resources at his command, Percival enquired about subsidiary occupations, and on seeing that only 10 per cent of the economically active declared one, thought that the result showed the extent and importance of secondary occupations to be very much less than had often been assumed – but he added that closer investigation was required. In 1960, 17 per cent of those working reported a secondary occupation, mostly males engaged in agriculture, and their second jobs were usually in construction, manufacturing, government service, and trade, and at the British military bases – virtually any work requiring sporadic, largely unskilled, labour, that is to say. Unfortunately the existence of secondary occupations could have led to inconsistency in reporting: a farmer who earned more ready cash from, say, blacksmithing than cultivating his crops, or who happened to be at the forge when the enumerator called, might easily misunderstand – even if he was told – the concept of the question, and report that he was a blacksmith, having said ten years earlier that he was a farmer. Even in the main occupation groups, therefore, the totals may not always be reliable.

The numbers of male workers in agriculture and production occupations, and their proportions in the economically active

| | Agricultural workers | | Production workers | |
	Total	Percentage	Total	Percentage
1911	49,700	64	11,400	15
1921	53,600	63	13,500	16
1931	55,300	56	16,900	17
1946	55,200	41	28,500	21
1960	43,300	26	54,300	34
1973*		16		39

* Non-Turkish-Cypriots only

male population, are cited first. 'Production workers', an abbreviated heading from the International Standard Classification of Occupations, includes, broadly, workers in manufacturing, processing and repairing.

Percival's contention that 'it is exceedingly hazardous to compare any two sets of figures describing the Cyprus farming community' was sound, but even so, two trends in these figures are clear; a striking diminution in the agricultural population, and a great – but not equally great – expansion in the numbers of production workers.

It was between 1931 and 1946 that the greatest number of persons ever was engaged in agriculture – probably just before the Second World War – but nevertheless, the *proportion* of male workers in agriculture had been falling since at least 1921 and probably earlier. New opportunities for work other than in agriculture must have been occurring quite early in the British period. In 1960 the true decrease in the proportion was certainly greater than shown and if the proportion was really 22 or 20 per cent instead of 26, it becomes clear that the main flight from agriculture took place between 1946 and 1960 – as the use of farm machinery was becoming common, and other jobs in large numbers were offering at the British bases. By 1973 no more than one in seven in the male labour force was engaged in agriculture – a remarkable change in the population's way of life in just over thirty years. At the same time production workers increased, but not because of any great expansion of industry, since the principal production occupations in 1960 were bricklayer; labourer; construction worker; mechanic and repairman; carpenter; shoe-maker; tailor – many of the trades required at the bases in fact. As the percentage of agricultural and production workers combined fell to 55 in 1973, what were the other jobs which then absorbed nearly half of all working males? They were chiefly those shown in the first set of figures opposite: a wide range of occupations, typical of a well-developed, if not highly industrialised, country, was now engaging the large proportion of working men which agriculture could no longer sustain.

According to the Turkish-Cypriot authorities, workers in the northern zone totalled 46,000 in 1977, or 32 per cent of the estimated total population (excluding Turkish military forces) –

	Percentages
Sales	10
Service	9
Clerical	8
Transport	8
Professional, technical	6

about the same proportion as reported in the south in 1973. A third of them, it was estimated, were females. Males and females together were engaged in broad industrial groups as follows:

	Percentages
Agriculture	51
Industry	12
Construction	7
Other	30

How accurate these statistics are is not known, but because industry is obviously less developed in the north than the south, the proportion of agricultural workers there must still be comparatively high.

In addition to the census-takers, the authors of two surveys have detailed the changing pattern of occupations. In Lysi village before 1946, some 80 per cent of workers were cultivators or shepherds, but by 1970 that percentage had fallen to about 23, and it would apparently decline still further in the future, as half of those working in agriculture were aged over 45. The principal new occupations were in the construction and other industries needing both skilled and unskilled labour, and as many as 35 per cent of the village's workers commuted to either Nicosia or Famagusta to do such jobs. In another village, surveyed by Loizos, only 10 per cent went off to the towns every day, but otherwise the transformation had been on similar lines (see overleaf). No doubt most villages could have told a similar story – plus an additional one of out-migration – over those decades.

The unbalanced age structure among agricultural workers in

	1925–35	1968–69
	Percentages	
Farmers	58	41
Shepherds	8	5
Muleteers	6	0
Civil servants	0	10
Car owners/drivers	0	10
Coffee-shop owners, retailers, etc.	4	12

Lysi was seen in the national censuses too. In 1946, 32 per cent of male agricultural workers, but only 17 per cent of non-agricultural workers, were aged 50 or over, and while the much greater differential in 1960 was biased by the inclusion in the economically active of elderly men helping out on the family smallholding, it was still clear that agriculture was being left largely to people in the older ages. In consequence, the occupations practised by men of different ages were far from identical:

	15–24	25 and over
	Percentages	
Production	48	29
Agricultural	13	31
Clerical	10	6
Service	7	9
Other	22	25
	100	100

It was the shift away from agricultural occupations which led to the author's being told in 1980 that the villages were now inhabited by the elderly, it was the wives who did much of the farming because the men had jobs in the towns, and it was not certain that enough labour could be found to work a large, valuable area of newly irrigated land.

'Although the educational standard of the Moslem Turks is rather below that of the Greek Orthodox, and although the Moslems as a whole are the rather more urban community, the occupational structure of the two communities is generally similar. Since each community is largely self-contained, there is scope even in the relatively small Turkish community for every kind of occupation . . . almost identical proportions of men in the two communities are engaged in farming, in catering and personal services, and even in commerce and the professions,' Percival observed in 1946. No further statistical information on the point has become available since then, but there is little reason to suppose that the situation differed greatly by 1964, when the two communities went their separate ways in regard to economic and every other activity.

A 1960 census table which was probably designed to define rural under-employment is of interest in suggesting how many persons then reported to be working in agriculture would not have been reckoned economically active at all in most other censuses. The question asked about work at any time in a specified week, it will be remembered, and the instruction to enumerators stated: 'Include part-time work such as Saturday job, helping in a farm, delivering newspapers. . . . If the person did any work at all during that week such as after school, Saturday or other part-time work, mark "Yes", even if it was for only one hour. . . . Many thousands of housewives, students and elderly persons do part-time work. Do not enter "No" for such persons without first being sure that they did not do any work at all.' Putting the onus on respondents to show that they had *not* worked was unusual, and while many people who contribute significantly to economic activity can be overlooked in censuses – and in Cyprus, many women in particular probably were – counting people working for only an hour in a week was out of line with other censuses, both in Cyprus and elsewhere. International usage is seen in the United Nations' suggestion of a minimum of one-third of normal working hours when it is necessary to decide whether workers in a family enterprise are, formally, economically active or not. Cyprus's 1960 table of rural employment in agriculture by duration indicates, then, how many agricultural workers reckoned as economically active would have been omitted by usual standards:

	Male	Female	Total
Total with agricultural occupations	47,568	39,457	87,025
Worked for 90 days or more	29,976	21,282	51,258
Worked for 120 days or more	26,084	15,961	42,045

The excess was about two-thirds for men, we see, and as much as 100 per cent for women. Allowing for some inaccuracy in recalling the number of days worked, the real totals by normal standards must have been in the region of:

Males	28,000
Females	18,500
Total	46,500

It is still difficult to assess how they compare with their equivalents in earlier censuses, since a somewhat different concept of time – of usual activity, i.e. not linked to a particular period – was then used, but the following new series of males and females together seems plausible:

1931	70,000
1946	63,400
1960	46,500
1973	26,700 (excluding Turkish-Cypriots)

Before leaving this topic, it may be noted that the total of 87,025 rural dwellers with agricultural occupations shown in the table of days worked is less than the numbers shown in other tables of rural occupations and industries; and, further, according to the main tables, most agricultural workers were females, while in that of days worked, men outnumbered women. In this table, then, the total appears incorrect, but because no other inconsistency is evident, it seems reasonable to accept the *pattern* of working days which it shows.

Employment status

Before 1946, 'no attempt was made to distinguish employers, workers on their own account and employees. This omission is unfortunate, since the distinction is of particular importance both socially and politically . . .' observed the 1946 census report, adding that its own data illustrated the extent to which the individual and small family business held the field both in commerce and in most manufacturing and service activities. The 1960 census did not provide useful comparisons, for reasons already discussed, but between 1946 and 1973 the proportion of employed persons increased rather slowly, and was no more than two-thirds of all workers at the latter date. Owing to the use of different classifications, comparisons are limited to those set out in Table 20. The categories omitted here, employer and own

TABLE 20: EMPLOYMENT STATUS, SELECTED CATEGORIES, 1946–73 (PERCENTAGES)

		Male	Female	Total
Employee	1946	?	?	58
	1960	58	35	51
	1973*	65	76	68
Unpaid family worker	1960	3	49	18
	1973*	1	12	3

* Excluding Turkish-Cypriots

account worker, together comprised (100−68−3=) 29 per cent of all workers in 1973. That this proportion was still so high – that so many working people were still their own masters – is a striking indication of the independence of Cypriot ideas when it comes to a job. In 1960, a useful cross-tabulation showed such people to be engaged mainly in the following occupations:

	Percentage
Farmers	54
Production workers	19
Sales workers	13

A stroll round any town today leaves one in no doubt about the continued importance of small enterprise in the Cypriot way of life.

Unemployment

'The unemployed . . . include persons who did not work during the time reference period but had looked for work. Simple as this definition may sound, the practical enumeration of this group entails several difficulties. . . .'[3] Before this warning was sounded by the United Nations, Percival had written in 1946: 'I would emphasize the great caution needed in assessing unemployment in a country where labour is so fluid and where agriculture and other occupations overlap so considerably as in Cyprus.' His enquiry on the subject was the first to be made on the island, and resulted in a figure of 3,436 persons in the non-agricultural sector – 4·4 per cent of the non-agricultural labour force. It was an unexpectedly high number at a time of apparent prosperity, he thought, but it had to be remembered that in November workers should have been back on their farms after the summer building and tourist season but not yet be too busy with farm work; also the Cyprus Regiment was being demobilised, and many ex-soldiers were still seeking work. From such problems in assessing unemployment we may conclude that census data about it are not always informative.[4] Certainly there is no obvious explanation of the contrasting figure of 58,387 unemployed given by the 1960 census – 25 per cent of the economically active population – nor was any provided in the census report.

Usually unemployment has not been a great problem. For instance, 1961, when 9,600 including newcomers to the labour force were registered as unemployed, was at a time of economic downturn and high emigration, but by 1966 only half as many were registered (excluding Turkish-Cypriots) – 1·4 per cent of the labour force. In 1972, when the total was 2,500, the registered unemployed were thought 'to have reached the minimum possible level consistent with the needs of a dynamic economy',[5] and at times there was a shortage of both skilled and unskilled workers. Two years later, after the Turkish occupation of the northern part of the island, 25,000 persons were registered as unemployed in the government-controlled area, and it was thought that as many again had not bothered to register – altogether some 25 per cent of the labour force. Yet that proportion fell to about 3 per cent by 1977, it was soon officially stated that some scarcity of skilled workers had developed into a general shortage of labour, and the author was told by one of the oldest manufacturers in 1980 that because enough workers were not available, plans for expansion had to be based on additional automation, and heard reference to the 'miracle' which had produced full employment so soon after 1974.

According to the Turkish-Cypriot authorities, the monthly average of unemployed was 2,470 in 1978[6] – about 5 per cent of the reported labour force. Nearly a quarter were aged under 20. Workers in the manufacturing, processing, and transport industries were the worst hit, something like 10 per cent of them apparently being out of work. A quarter of the unemployed normally worked in agriculture, it was stated, but as their monthly numbers multiplied several times during the year for some reason which is not obvious, some lack of consistency in collecting the data seems likely.

In summary, the pattern of individuals' occupations has changed fundamentally in the last four decades; an indication is quickly seen in the following ratios of male workers in agriculture and production:

1931   3·3 agriculture : 1 production
1973   1 agriculture : 2·5 production

Transport, sales and service occupations have grown, and in the whole process an unusually large proportion of men have remained their own masters, either as employers or working on their own. Women, who have always worked in agriculture, are increasingly taking paid jobs, competing with men for them on level terms. Secondary occupations are probably still common, particularly among farmers. Unemployment, and particularly under-employment, have been considerable at times, but today are minimal in the south, while the former is reported to be at a moderate level in the north. A number of reasons have enabled the transformation in work patterns to be unusually rapid, among them the coincidence after the Second World War of the mechanisation of agriculture, the opportunity of alternative jobs at, or connected with, the British bases and in the expanded government and commercial fields, new levels of affluence, and the possibility for many people of commuting from their rural homes to non-agricultural work. Less direct but fundamentally important influences in the transition have been, we may think: the small size of the island, which both made commuting possible and led to the rapid transmission of new ideas, for instance concerning agricultural methods; the avidity for education which prepared people for the new jobs at professional, technical and skilled levels; a spirit of personal enterprise; and the tradition of concern for the family which has always encouraged parents to give their children, first, the best possible schooling, and, second, the best inheritance they can provide.

8

THE FUTURE

SINCE the population's growth rate has undergone a radical change in a mere twenty-five years, it cannot be assumed that in the future it will either remain constant or continue to change in the same fashion. Consequently, estimates of the population's future size must be based on detailed measures – the most plausible levels of fertility, mortality and migration. This chapter contains the results of projections so calculated, while the Appendix gives details of the method. A projection is not a forecast, it should be noted, but a statement of how the population will grow if the assumptions concerning fertility, mortality and migration which have been used continue to be valid.

The calculated totals for the non-Turkish-Cypriot population, with the proportions in broad age groups, are shown in Table 21. In the twenty-five-year period, the population will increase by 20 per cent, but far from evenly, the increase in the final quinquen-

TABLE 21: PROJECTED POPULATION (EXCLUDING TURKISH-CYPRIOTS), 1976–2001 – TOTAL NUMBERS, AND PROPORTIONS IN BROAD AGE GROUPS

	1976	1981	1986	1991	1996	2001
			(thousands)			
Total	496	517	542	565	583	596
			(percentages)			
0–14	26	24	24	25	24	23
15–34	35	36	34	30	28	27
35–59	25	26	28	30	33	35
60 and over	14	14	14	15	15	15
	100	100	100	100	100	100

nium being 13,000, while in the first it amounted to 21,000. The annual growth rates implied are:

	Per cent
1976–80	0·87
1981–85	0·93
1986–90	0·84
1991–95	0·64
1996–2001	0·44

In the quarter of a century preceding 1976, the growth rate of the Greek-Cypriot community – virtually the population being projected – fell continuously from about 1·5 to some 0·7 per cent per year, but now we foresee two quite different, apparently inconsistent, features in the future: a sizeable upturn in the rate in the first years, followed in the final five-year period by a much lower level than Cyprus has experienced for at least a century.

The reason for this surprising variation – within the 1990s alone, the rate will actually fall by nearly a half – can be traced back to the highly uneven age distributions of recent years, such as the following in 1960:

	Females
5–9	33,172
10–14	32,843
15–19	24,212
20–24	24,443

After allowing for some inaccuracy in reporting ages, the unevenness of these groups reflects two separate influences which happened to coincide: the post-war increase in fertility experienced in many countries, and a high level of age-selective emigration. The former led to a 'bulge' in the population aged about 10–14 in 1960, while the latter removed large numbers of people from the population, particularly those in the younger working ages, causing a dip in the numbers aged over 15. During the succeeding decade, the females aged 15–24 in 1960 were having their children, and because they were comparatively few in numbers, their children were fewer too; and at the same time fertility was falling. In consequence the growth rate also fell. By about 1978, however, the girls aged 10–14 in 1960 were having their children, and since there were more of them, their children also were more numerous, and the rate rose again. We see that it will remain at what is, on recent form, quite a high level for about fifteen years, but will fall again when those smaller numbers of children born in the 1960s and early 1970s are themselves having their children in the mid and late 1990s. During the following generation – beyond the period of these projections – the same cycle will repeat itself, although the tendency will be for the variations in growth to lessen as time goes on.

The progress of the diminished age groups as they become older can be discerned in Table 21. That the proportions of children and the elderly will differ little over twenty-five years is a mark of a population which is reaching stability of fertility and mortality, but the greatly varying proportions in the two middle groups are due to the ageing of the children of those groups which were deficient in size around 1960. The cause of the low rate foreseen for the turn of the century is now obvious: persons aged 15–34, who include the great majority of the women having children, will be, proportionately to the whole population, no more than three-quarters of their numbers twenty years earlier. A few years later still, the proportions of the over-60 group will increase a little. The number of the very elderly – persons aged 75 and over – will grow somewhat faster than either the total population or even the whole over-60 group throughout the projection period and for some time thereafter, because people who are very elderly today have lived through times when mortality was much higher than today, so comparatively large numbers of their contemporaries have died; in twenty years' time, however, they will have lived through longer periods of lower mortality, so larger numbers will survive.

The distortions of age distribution have unexpected effects when particular sections of the population, the economically active and more especially the school children, are considered. Details are shown in Table 22. A notable instance is that the number of children of primary school age in 2001 will be almost

TABLE 22: PROJECTED SCHOOL AND ECONOMICALLY
ACTIVE POPULATIONS (EXCLUDING TURKISH-
CYPRIOTS), 1976–2001

| | School | | Economically active | | |
	Primary	Secondary	Male	Female	Total
1976	49,900	52,800	124,900	42,500	167,400
1981	44,900	45,700	137,400	45,200	182,600
1986	49,300	40,500	149,200	46,500	195,700
1991	55,300	43,300	156,800	45,900	202,700
1996	57,400	49,700	163,000	46,600	209,600
2001	50,200	53,100	169,500	48,600	218,100

the same as it was in 1976, despite total population growth of 20
per cent. These children are reckoned to be all those aged 6 to 11
inclusive. (The proportions aged 6–9 and 10–11 in the relevant
quinquennial groups have been adopted from the 1973 census.)
Naturally, the actual numbers of children attending primary
school will be somewhat larger, owing to some need to repeat
classes, and in fact in 1978–79, 54,200 children were in primary
school,[1] but of that number, 48,000 were aged 6 to 11 – a
reasonable correspondence with our projected numbers.
However, the main point of interest is the peculiar pattern of the
projected totals. At two periods, the Ministry of Education will
have an unusual problem on its hands – contracting numbers of
primary pupils and a lessening requirement for primary school
teachers.

When secondary school pupils are considered, an element of
estimation must be introduced, since not all children of secondary
school age attend school, nor are they likely to within the
projection period. Because the percentage of the estimated
number of children aged 12–17 actually attending school in
1978–79 was as high as 83, it might not be affected much by any
extension of compulsory schooling within the projection period;
consequently we assume only a modest increase in that proportion in each quinquennium – 1 per cent. That the first and final
secondary school figures are as close to each other as in the case of
primary school age children is a coincidence, because although an

156

uneven pattern is to be expected again, it should occur six years later. In fact it does, so looking further ahead, we conclude that by the year 2006 the number of secondary pupils will fall considerably from the total of 53,100 in 2001. The whole school-going population will decrease to a low point of about 90,000 by the mid-1980s, and will rise rapidly over the next decade to 107,000 – an interesting illustration of the long-term effects which unusual demographic features leave behind them.

The economically active population, on the other hand, will increase steadily, since, encompassing a much wider age range, it is less subject to irregularities of age distribution. Estimating it entails an element of judgment again, because the proportions of workers in the population may vary, and in the case of females they are difficult to measure now, let alone foresee in the future. However, there is no reason to think that the proportions, male and female, found in 1973 were unreasonable or will change radically – although the use in future of another definition of 'economically active' could result in very different numbers, as actually happened in 1960. To project the numbers of the economically active, those proportions have been applied to the five-year groups of males and females separately from 15 to 64 years at each stage of the projection. By the year 2001, 36 per cent more men than in 1976 will be wanting jobs – a greater increase than that of the total population. If, as seems likely, the opportunities for work in agriculture will grow by only a few thousand as irrigation schemes are extended up to the clear limits now thought feasible, most of them must presumably be found in the non-agricultural sector. The future demands for work by women are more difficult to gauge, because they are subject to non-demographic factors such as women's increasing freedom to take paid jobs, but perhaps it may be envisaged, in broad terms, that more women will seek such work in the future, while smallholding agriculture will at least maintain its present demands on rural women; in sum, that the proportion of working women will rise rather than fall, and that the numbers of economically active women projected may err on the low side.

(That the uncertainties of what constitutes 'economic activity' in Cyprus' statistics are not yet resolved is seen by comparing the 202,900 persons economically active in 1976 according to the *Economic Report 1978* (Table 33) with our 167,400 in the same

year. The discrepancy apparently stems from differing definitions, which caused the 1973 census to find 166,400 economically active persons, while two years later the total was 207,300
according to the *Economic Report*. As the total population was
officially estimated to be less in 1975 than in 1973, the
economically active population could not have increased by
about 25 per cent in the same time. In the absence of stated
definitions, the accuracy of such figures cannot be assessed, but
one divergence, in the numbers engaged in agriculture, may be
noted – 26,700 from the 1973 census, but 43,900 in 1975
according to the *Economic Report*. It is because the active
proportions in each sex-age group in 1973 appear reasonable
that they have been used in the projection.)

Because assumptions concerning future fertility, mortality and
migration are never certain, projections are customarily made in
two or more alternative versions, in the expectation that actual
growth will lie somewhere between them. The United Nations,
for instance, calculates high, medium, and low variants, in which
the first and last 'are intended to represent the upper and lower
boundaries of a zone of greatest plausibility', while the 'medium
estimates are those appearing most likely in the light of past
experience and present circumstances'. High and low variants
can vary considerably – for instance by as much as 9 per cent at
the end of twenty-five years in one country near to Cyprus,
according to the United Nations. This approach is not adopted
here, for two reasons. As explained earlier, the fertility and
mortality of the non-Turkish-Cypriot population cannot change
much in the future in the absence of exceptional circumstances,
and any small fluctuations will have litttle effect on total
population size. Secondly, in such conditions the remaining
factor, migration, can become the most important variable – and
in Cyprus, its volume is unforeseeable. Consequently there is no
point in making alternative projections based on slightly different
fertility and mortality levels, when the effects of such variations
can be far outweighed by unpredictable amounts of migration.

In this respect, Cyprus is in an unusual position, for in most
countries migration is the minor factor. To emphasise it, a second
projection has been calculated, using the same assumptions about
fertility and mortality, but assuming zero migration. It serves
primarily to show the effect of migration on future population

growth; but as zero net migration is not outside the bounds of possibility, its usefulness may not be entirely theoretical. The results follow, line A being copied from Table 21, and line B being the new projection.

	1976	1981	1986	1991	1996	2001
			(thousands)			
A	496	517	542	563	583	596
B	496	522	553	583	608	629

Since the original projection, line A, assumes net migration of 1,000 persons per year, it must total at least 25,000 persons less than line B in the year 2001; the difference is actually 33,000, because line B includes not only those 25,000 non-emigrants but the children to be born to them up to 2001 as well. More significantly, the difference increases at each stage, being 2 per cent in 1986, 4 per cent in 1996, and 6 per cent in 2001. Even in Cyprus, net emigration of 1,000 persons a year arouses little interest, but here it is seen that that outflow will have a marked effect on population size in a generation, that after two generations it will be much greater, and so on into the future. As stated earlier, the figure of 1,000 net emigrants per year is hypothetical; the true figure could just as well be 2,000 as zero. If it really were 2,000 – not at all impossible, on past form – the loss of population after twenty-five years would be not 6 but 12 per cent – a notable proportion in any country.

The proportions in age groups shown in Table 21 are also valid (with two negligible exceptions) for the projection which takes no account of migration – line B above – so that the numbers of persons in those groups and in the school-going ages and the labour force according to the new projection can easily be calculated by applying the same proportions to the totals in line B.

No projection of the Turkish-Cypriot population has been made, in the absence both of demonstrably reliable information on its present size and on fertility and mortality. If a guess about future years were to be hazarded, it might be on the lines that the small differential in the Cypriot Greek and Turkish growth rates before 1960 – the latter being the higher – has probably continued, and could have increased as the Greek rate fell in the 1960s; Turkish natural growth might well have been at 1 per cent or more a year in the last two decades. On the other hand, it is possible that Turkish fertility and mortality have been affected by political and economic conditions since 1964, resulting, perhaps, in a falling rate of natural growth. For the near future, it seems possible – but is not certain – that natural increase will still be at a higher rate than among the Greek-Cypriots. The factor of migration cannot be foreseen at all on the information now available.

In general terms, Cyprus' future population growth should bring few of the problems experienced in many other countries – the need to provide large numbers of new jobs as the labour force grows rapidly, for example, or the drain on national resources which can be brought about by educating a burgeoning school-age population. Indeed, concern could rather be concentrated on the *low* rate of growth, and it is possible to envisage consideration of a policy, not of family limitation, but of encouraging larger families, perhaps by means such as increased family allowances and longer paid maternity leave. This does not imply that Cyprus, with its apparently limited natural resources, will easily support a greatly enlarged population in the future; but political considerations – which are outside the scope of this study – will doubtless enter into any population policy. What Attalides termed Cyprus' relatively unique opportunity of exporting its surplus labour in significant proportions will probably continue to exist, although on a smaller scale than at certain times in the past; if the position of near-full employment today deteriorates in future, the outflow which would have resulted earlier will be restricted to some extent by the growing reluctance of the countries with Cypriot communities, notably England, to accept new immigrants. A significant inflow of immigrants into Cyprus seems unlikely; it is returning emigrants who could add considerably to the population, but they have not done so in the last century, and at present there is little reason to foresee that they will in the future. In the long term, migration may well become a less important factor in population growth, which, dependent largely on low levels of fertility and mortality, would then stabilise at a very low rate. Just how low that rate will be in comparison with neighbouring countries may be seen by comparing the projected rates for

Cyprus with the following cited by the United Nations for the period 1975–2000: Egypt, 2·6 per cent per year, falling to 2·0 per cent; Lebanon, 2·4–1·9 per cent; Syria, 3·2–2·9 per cent; Turkey, 2·5–1·7 per cent.[2] An easy way to grasp the contrast presented by such figures is to compare the number of years needed for each population to double in size: they are, very approximately, Egypt, 30 years; Lebanon, 32 years; Syria, 23 years; Turkey, 35 years – and Cyprus, 100 years. Cyprus's demographic progress is out of line with its neighbours, it is seen, and is European in pattern; as may be expected, it is similar to that of Greece, where growth is foreseen to be 0·5–0·6 per cent a year, implying a doubling time of about 125 years.

In conclusion, it may be remembered that population growth in Cyprus has had a chequered history. Before 1878, the predominant influences were non-demographic, at least for long periods; from 1878 to the mid-1950s, the chief factors were the natural ones of fertility and mortality, so growth then followed a recognisable long-term pattern; in the following twenty years, non-demographic influences were again of great importance, and were accompanied by exceptionally rapid falls in fertility and mortality. With massive emigration due to a political emergency having occurred as recently as 1974, it would be unwise to rule out further non-demographic influences in the future, but barring their re-emergence, population growth in the years to come will return to the steady pattern of the early decades of this century. However, the pace will be rather slower, and the age distribution better-balanced in that the workers in the population will much more nearly equal the non-workers – bearing, in fact, all the marks of a demographically well-developed society.

APPENDIX

DEFINITIONS AND ANALYSIS

THIS Appendix details certain techniques and definitions which, though forming an integral part of the analysis described in Chapters 5 to 8, may be of lesser interest to some readers of this study. It is for their convenience that they are placed separately in an Appendix.

Mortality

Mortality levels from 1891 to 1931 were estimated by projecting the age groups at each census forward over a ten-year period, using various levels in the South series of Coale and Demeny's model life tables, and comparing the results with the population aged 10 and overnumerated at the following census. Two preliminary adjustments were made. Firstly, quinquennial age groups were smoothed by the formula $1/16 \, (- S_{-2} + 4S_{-1} + 10S + 4S_1 - S_2)$ suggested by the United Nations. Secondly, because of apparent inconsistencies in the two youngest age groups, the numbers in them were redistributed according to an appropriate model population. Further, net emigration was reckoned to total:

1901–10	4,000 persons
1911–20	5,000 persons
1921–30	5,500 persons

Levels after 1931 were estimated from the census questions asked of females in 1946, 1960 and 1973 about the numbers of children they had borne and the numbers still alive. As experience elsewhere shows that such enquiries are not always answered accurately, the detail of Cyprus' questions is worth examining first. In 1946 the questions read: '(Only married, widowed and divorced women are to answer this question.) How many live children in all have you given birth to?' and 'How many of your children are still alive?' As there was no instruction about the manner of asking the questions, we do not know whether

162

enumerators were alerted to their particular pitfalls, nor how many householders answered them without the help of an enumerator. In 1960 the wording was: 'For women only – how many children in all have you given birth to; how many of your children are still living?' – differing from the 1946 questions in two significant respects: first, the questions were addressed to all women, ever-married or not; second, the word 'live' was omitted. Could these points impair the comparability of the results? They could, but probably did not. The unusual extension of the enquiry to all women was apparently inadvertent, as the enquiry 'How many times were you married?' was also to be asked of all women including those who had just stated that they were unmarried. It seems safe to suppose that most enumerators realised that the question was muddled, and refrained from putting it to women who had never married. The omission of 'live' – which opened the way to including still-births in the number of children born – was counteracted by an instruction to enumerators that still-births should be excluded; what was required for the first part of the questions was 'all live children whether born of the present marriage or previous marriages and whether legitimate or illegitimate'. Precise though this wording is, it is still prudent to remember that these questions have proved susceptible to error elsewhere. To draw on the author's own experience: 'it was found at the trial enumeration that a few enumerators consistently recorded the same answers to both questions because they failed to grasp the difference between them . . . Where the enumerator erred, he had not understood that the answer to the first question should include children who had died.'[1]

Owing to the tendency of respondents to overlook, or at least fail to report, dead children, incorrect response to these two questions leads to an underestimate of mortality. However, in Cyprus certain considerations suggest that the answers to them may have been comparatively accurate. Firstly, fertility was not very high by world standards, so respondents' propensity to overlook babies born long ago should not have been excessive. Secondly, because standards of education were comparatively high, that propensity, usually commonest among the illiterate, should again have been small. Thirdly, illegitimate children being rare in Cyprus, reluctance on the part of unmarried mothers to declare their children hardly came into question. Fourthly, in reporting the results of these questions, Percival apparently assumed them to be correct. Even though he could not have realised all the possibilities of error described in later demographic literature, it seems inconceivable that he overlooked blatant inaccuracies in the answers. All in all, error was probably minimal in 1946 and 1960. As for 1973, no information on which to make any assessment is available.

The mortality of children born alive, cross-classified by mother's ages, is summarised in Table 23. A number of points may be noted here. Mortality clearly fell between 1946 and 1973,

TABLE 23: SURVIVAL OF CHILDREN BORN ALIVE TO MOTHERS IN SELECTED AGE GROUPS, 1946–73

	Percentage survivors of children born alive to mothers aged*						
	20–24	25–34	35–44	45–54	55–64	14–44	45+
1946							
Cyprus	89	86	81	75	68	83	70
Greek Ortho-dox	?	?	?	74		84	72
Moslem	?	?	?	63		80	61
1960							
Cyprus	95	92	88	83	?	91	76
6 towns	97	94	89	84	?	93	81
Rural	94	91	87	81	?	89	75
1973							
Non-Turkish-Cypriots	98	97	94	91	86	95	84

* The age groups are those given in 1946

both in infancy and throughout life: the children of women aged 55–64, for instance, were probably in their thirties at the time of the enumeration, and the proportion surviving increased by 18 per cent. In 1946 the gap between the survivors to mothers in the youngest and the older age groups was considerably larger than in 1973 – suggesting that even by 1946 infant mortality had already fallen. Confirmation of this decline is seen in the figures for women aged 20–24, all of whose children must still have been young: that the increase in survival was higher in the earlier years also suggests that it had begun well before 1946. Where different sections of the community were tabulated, some differential was always found. Data for the Greek Orthodox and Moslems were given only in 1946, and clearly suggested that earlier, before 1930 probably, mortality among Moslems had been notably higher, but that the differential was disappearing. The 1960 census showed mortality to be lower in urban than rural areas, but the difference was small, and it probably had little significance, because by 1960 the dividing line between urban and rural life-styles was becoming blurred by migration. Many urban women aged over 45, for instance, must have had their children in rural areas before they moved to the towns.

If successive censuses become more efficient, as often occurs, the underestimates of mortality due to inaccurate reporting become smaller, and consequently the proportions reported dead can even increase from one census to the next, simply because error had decreased. A suggestion that such a bias exists in Cyprus is seen by comparing the proportions of children reported surviving by cohorts of women at successive censuses. One example follows:

Census of	Age of women	Percentage surviving
1946	20–24	88·9
1960	35–39	90·3
1973	45–49	92·3

The percentage can actually increase between censuses if the women are of child-bearing age and continue to have children, more of whom survive; but after the child-bearing period, it cannot increase, and it will certainly decrease, because some of the children surviving at the earlier census will have died in the interval before the next. Consequently, the increase shown here between 1946 and 1960 is possibly correct, but as not many Cypriot women over the age of 35–39 have babies, the continued increase up to 1973 is suspect. It cannot be designated as clearly incorrect, because the female populations at the two dates were not quite the same – in 1973, the Turkish-Cypriots were excluded, and further, numbers of the women enumerated in 1960 had emigrated; but even so, some suspicion about it seems justified. However, this pattern is not consistent in all cohorts, so it is not possible to conclude firmly that the questions were generally answered more accurately in 1946 than 1973.

A different test can be made by comparing the average numbers of children dead per mother by cohorts of mothers at successive censuses. Unlike the proportion of children dying to a cohort of women still in the child-bearing ages, the number of children dead per mother can never decrease. A comparison of the 1946 and 1960 data, limited to two cohorts because of the size of the groups tabulated in 1946 and the long interval before the next census, yields the expected result of more children dead per mother in 1960. On this score, there is no reason to suppose that one census was less efficient than the other. However, the 1960 and 1973 data reveal patterns of children dead which differ in the younger and older groups. Because the interval was approximately twelve years and three months, the numbers of children dead per mother in 1973 have been obtained by summing the numbers of mothers, children born alive and children dead in the appropriate two quinquennial age groups of mothers and dividing the totals by two. Equally, the same procedure could have been applied to the 1960 data instead (to obtain age groups of mothers beginning with 17·5–22·5 instead of 20–24 years), but using this alternative does not, in fact, affect the conclusion to be drawn. Details of the comparison follow:

1960		1973	
20–24	0·60	32·5–37·5	0·15
25–29	0·18	37·5–42·5	0·21
30–34	0·29	42·5–47·5	0·27
35–39	0·40	47·5–52·5	0·37
40–44	0·60	52·5–57·5	0·50
45–49	0·71	57·5–62·5	0·63
50 and over	1·35	62·5 and over	1·12

Unlike mothers aged 20–29, those aged 30 and over in 1960 gave *smaller* numbers at the later census, on a scale which grew with increasing age. Mothers aged 50 and over in 1960 actually reported 20 per cent fewer children dead in 1973. Clearly, there is a suggestion of consistently inaccurate reporting in the latter year by mothers aged more than 40 or so, but again, the exclusion of the Turkish-Cypriots in 1973 means that the population enumerated by the two censuses are not wholly comparable. If, as now seems probable, there was some weakness in the 1973 data, it took the form mainly of understatement of the numbers of children born. Fertility measures derived from the data would, then, be slightly underestimated. As far as mortality is concerned, calculated levels would be too high and calculated death rates too low.

The proportions of children who have died can be converted into conventional mortality measures by a method originally devised by Brass and subsequently elaborated by others, including the United States National Academy of Sciences, whose method is used here. Brass-type estimates of childhood mortality are shown to pertain to some particular period life table at certain times in the past; it thus takes account of changing mortality such as has occurred in Cyprus. A factor (k) is applied to the proportion dead reported by women in each quinquennial group to give the probability of dying before a certain childhood age (q); the numbers of survivors to this age (l) are then compared with model life tables, and the appropriate mortality levels are read off. A separate factor (t) then estimates the interval between the census date and the time at which the childhood mortality estimate was representative. An example of these calculations, using the 1960 data for the whole population, follows:

Age group of females	Proportion dead	$k(i)$	Age x	$q(x)$	$l(x)$	Mortality level	$t(i)$
20–24	·0545	1·1120	2	·0606	·9374	19	1·85
25–29	·0659	1·0257	3	·0676	·9324	19	3·64
30–34	·0815	1.0223	5	·0833	·9167	19	6·27
35–39	·1026	1·0353	10	·1062	·8938	18	8·47
40–44	·1292	1·0219	15	·1320	·8680	17	11·26
45–49	·1504	1·0143	20	·1526	·8474	16	14·29

THE POPULATION OF CYPRUS

The models used are those of Coale and Demeny, in which level 18, to give one example, implies life expectancy of 62·5 years for females and 58·5 years for males. In this instance, that level would have been representative of a time 8·47 years before the 1960 census, i.e. mid-1952. Since the earliest time thus indicated is 11·7 years before the 1946 census, i.e. mid-1935, a series of mortality levels at frequent intervals from 1935 to 1971 is obtained.

The levels and life expectancies which we have calculated from 1891 on are:

| | Level | | Life expectancy | |
	Male	Female	Male	Female
1891–1900	9	8	39	38
1901–10	12	11	45	45
1911–20	12	12½	46	49
1921–30	13	13	47	50
1935–39		13	47	50
1940–46		15	52	55
1947–51		17	56	60
1952–56		19	61	65
1957–60		19	61	65
1961–65		20	63·5	67·5
1966–69		21	66	70
1970–71		23	71	75

The series appears generally plausible, except perhaps at the turn of the century. If net emigration from 1901 to 1910 amounted to 2,000, not 4,000, persons, the calculated levels for that decade would be 11 (males) and 10 (females) and the progression smoother, but which number was the more accurate cannot be known now. That male expectancy was then higher than, or equal to, female expectancy seems unusual today, but could have been explained by factors such as the risks of childbirth which decreased later; smaller regard, possibly, for girl children; and the status of women in general. The last point was noted by an early British doctor: Cypriot men were fine, straight fellows, but the women were much inferior, because, he thought, they were comparatively poorly fed, they constantly carried children about and they did not only all the household drudgery but more than their fair share of work at harvest time as well. At the final date, 1970, expectancy of 71–75 years was higher than that of the United Kingdom and the United States – not proving that they were overestimated, certainly, but also not contradicting the suggestion made earlier that the calculated levels might be too high.

The number of deaths in each inter-censal period is now calculated by, firstly, applying the quinquennial survival ratios appropriate to the calculated mortality levels to the population at one census and subtracting the result in the next census year from the original population. Secondly, the number of births during the inter-censal period and the deaths occurring to them are calculated by the reverse survival method, using the appropriate age groups in the second census. The two totals of deaths are added together. Since the populations are tabulated in, and the survival ratios are applicable to, five-year groups, the numbers of deaths may be calculated for each five-year period separately. The five-year total is divided by five to give the annual average, and that average is assumed to be the number of deaths in the central year of the period. The crude death rate for that year is obtained by comparing the number of deaths with the estimated total population.

Up to 1931 the results of this process were satisfactory, but thereafter appeared to be less reliable. An example, using the 1931 and 1946 data, is given overleaf.

Here, the 1931 age groups have been smoothed, but not those of 1946 because the age distribution of the population was then distorted by age-selective emigration anyway.[2] It is emigration which makes the surprising excess of some 15,000 in the enumerated population even more unexpected, for if some 5,000 people emigrated in the inter-censal period, the enumerated population should have been less than our calculated population by that number, not 15,000 in excess. It seems that 20,000 extra people somehow entered the enumerated population by 1946.

Considering the quinquennial age groups reveals two points of interest. The first is found in most inter-censal periods – a shortage in the enumerated population between 25 and 45 years of age. We may be confident that it results from emigration. The

	1931 Population		Calculated 1946 population		Enumerated 1946 population	
	M	F	M	F	M	F
0–4	21,816	20,815				
5–9	19,002	18,315				
10–14	19,036	18,302				
15–19	17,748	18,412	20,079	19,016	21,367	22,220
20–24	15,242	16,954	17,391	17,263	18,906	19,440
25–29	12,716	14,412	17,846	17,057	15,412	16,952
30–34	11,337	12,096	16,229	16,909	15,286	15,743
35–39	10,094	10,290	13,721	15,364	13,665	14,987
40–44	8,800	9,231	11,234	12,888	11,640	12,252
45–49	8,449	8,589	9,739	10,646	11,163	11,778
50–54	7,741	7,631	8,321	8,845	9,532	9,987
55–59	6,355	6,102	6,827	7,624	7,453	7,449
60 & over	14,378	14,101	16,920	18,775	20,724	22,144
All ages	172,714	175,250	138,307	144,387	145,148	152,952

second, however, is peculiar to this one inter-censal period: over half of the unexpected excess in the enumerated population is in the ages 15–24 – among people who were under 10 in 1931, that is to say. Since under-enumeration of young children is not uncommon, were some under-10s omitted in 1931? The pattern of the youngest age groups in that year, viz.:

0–4	39,372
5–9	40,563
10–14	36,311
15–19	37,399

suggests that either age reporting was seriously inaccurate or that numbers of young children were overlooked. There is, then, good reason for thinking that much of the excess of 8,000 was due to under-enumeration of very young children in 1931. If this point is accepted, the overall excess should more correctly be in the region of 12,000. Reasons for it cannot be identified precisely, but two factors of possible relevance may be mentioned. Firstly, the method of selecting the model life tables used is based on infant mortality data; consequently, if survival at older ages in Cyprus were relatively better than in the youngest years, the calculated older populations would be deficient. Secondly, the marked difference in quality between the 1931 and 1946 censuses described in Chapter 2 leads to suspicion that under-enumeration in the former year was not confined to young children, but could have extended throughout the whole population; if such were the case, the calculated population in 1946 would again be too small. It is quite possible that both reasons together help to explain further the general excess in the enumerated population in 1946. One more point remains to be considered – the large excess in the oldest group enumerated, 60 and over. Here, it is easy to suspect some inaccuracy in the reporting of their ages by older people, since even in 1946 many of them could hardly have known how old they were to within a few years.

Fertility

Crude birth rates from 1894 have been calculated by the reverse survival method. Up to 1931, three preliminary adjustments to the base data were made: the age groups were smoothed, as described earlier; half the population aged 10 was reckoned to be under 10 (because of the preference for round numbers and the uncertainty of exact ages experienced in other countries and seen later in Cyprus); and under-enumeration of 2 per cent in the 0–9 age group was assumed. In total, the adjustments were sizeable, as the following instance from 1921 shows:

	Census		Adjusted	
	Male	Female	Male	Female
0–4	18,263	17,096	21,803	20,990
5–9	19,912	19,630	19,104	18,390
	38,175	36,726	40,907	39,380

After 1931 not only was the South series of model life tables used, but also the West tables arranged in single years instead of quinquennial groups, because rapid changes in fertility levels such as have occurred in Cyprus should be more accurately reflected in the application of survival ratios to, say, the numbers of children aged 0, 1, 2, 3 and 4 separately rather than to the group 0–4.

A summary of the answers to the question on the numbers of children born alive to women is given in Table 24. Between 1946 and 1973 an overall decline in fertility is obvious, yet in the reproductive ages women reported more children in 1960 than in 1946 – suggesting an upsurge in fertility in the years 1930–45. By 1973, a very marked fall in every group was to be found. Was it more emphasised in one section of the population than another? In 1946, Greek women were having fewer children than Moslem women, we see, but even more important was the urban–rural differential, at least in the only year when it was tabulated, 1960. Over the age of 25, urban women in the reproductive years were having 25 to 30 per cent less children than rural women; and over the age of 45, the differential was as great, or greater.

Since few women anywhere bear children at any age over 45, the line '45 and over' indicates the completed family size. It is seen

TABLE 24: AVERAGE NUMBER OF CHILDREN BORN ALIVE PER WOMAN, IN SELECTED AGE GROUPS, 1946, 1960 AND 1973

	1946	1960	1973*	1946 Greek Orth.	Moslem	1960 Urban	Rural
25–34	2·1	2·5	1·8			2·0	2·7
35–44	3·7	3·8	3·3			3·0	4·3
45–54	4·5	4·1	3·8			3·1	4·6
65 +	5·3	4·7	4·3			3·9†	5·0†
15–44	1·8	2·0	1·5	1·7	2·1	1·7	2·2
45 +	4·9	4·4	4·0	4·9	4·9	3·4	4·8

* Excluding Turkish-Cypriots
† 60 and over
Note: The age groups are those given in the 1946 census tabulations

to have fallen from 4·9 to 4·0 between 1946 and 1973, i.e. by 18 per cent. But although the completed family at the later date had four children and two of them must, on average, have been daughters, the gross reproduction rate in that year – the number of daughters born to women experiencing the age-specific fertility rates shown for 1973 – was only 1·13. This apparent contradiction is a reminder that the gross reproduction rate measures current fertility, whereas the completed family size in 1973 applied to women who were having most of their children at least fifteen years earlier, that is before 1958, and in the case of some of them, as far back as 1930. Here is an implication that fertility could have been falling before the Second World War. Further, it is seen from the lines '45–54' and '65 and over' that the older women always reported a larger completed family size than those who had had their children more recently. Some irregularity in the numbers of children reported at these ages is not unusual – but in the reverse direction; because older women tend to overlook babies born long ago, particularly those who died young, over the age of 45 the number of children said to have been born can *fall* in successively older age groups. That these

173

numbers actually rise with older age in Cyprus – quite consistently, it is seen from the census tabulations – suggests that forgetfulness was small, and that fertility indeed fell at the time in question. Remembering that the peak reproductive periods of women aged 45–54 and 65 and over in 1946 were from 1911 to 1935 and from 1900 or earlier to 1915 respectively, we see a strong indication in Table 24 that fertility was falling very early in this century.

The data on the numbers of children born alive were used to indicate fertility in another way – by differencing the average numbers born to a cohort at successive censuses. For example, because the 25–34 group of women had borne an average of 2·1 children in 1946 and in 1960 almost the same group, then aged 40–49, had had an average of 4·0 children (according to detailed data not shown here), they had an average of 1·9 children per woman in the intervening period. This is an age-specific rate, less informative than those derived from registration data because it applies to a broad age group over a period as long as fourteen years, yet having the advantage of being based on a source independent of vital registration. Since the first inter-censal period was fourteen years and the age groups spanned ten years, the numbers of children reported born in 1946 were first re-arranged in ten-year groups of women aged 16–25 etc.; the fourteen-year fertility rates were then obtained by comparing the numbers reported by the same cohorts at the two dates; and the results were pro-rated down to ten-year rates. For the later period 1960–73 – when the interval between the censuses was actually 12 years, 3 months and 20 days, but was reckoned as 12·5 years – the numbers reported born to women in quinquennial groups in 1960 were pro-rated to 1963 and then compared with the numbers calculated to have been reported by the same cohorts in 1973; that is to say, the group 22·5–27·5 years in 1963 was compared with that aged 32·5–37·5 in 1973. The combination of long inter-censal periods and wide age groups produces results within the groups which are not very informative – for example, within the 25–34 cohort in 1946, the younger women must have had more than 1·9 children and the older women fewer; and further, the births were certainly not evenly spaced over such a span of time – but the gross reproduction rates derived from the sums of these individual rates in 1960 and 1973 should be reliable. Those now obtained are: 1960, 2·39; 1973, 1·24.

The classification since 1950 of births by age of mother makes it possible to calculate annual age-specific fertility rates – the number of children born to 1,000 women in each age group – after estimating the female population by linear interpolation between censuses. Such rates have the advantage of independence of variations in the age-structure of a population and – particularly important in the context of Cyprus – of distortions in that structure resulting from emigration. The sum of the age-specific rates gives a total fertility rate – the total number of children which would be born to a group of women if the group passed through its reproductive life with these birth rates at each age – and also the gross reproduction rate – a standard measure, indicating the number of daughters which would be born to a group of women under the same circumstances (assuming in this case that the sex ratio of births is 105 males: 100 females).[3] These rates depend on the accuracy of vital registration, so it follows that if registration in one year were deficient by, say, 10 per cent, the total fertility and gross reproduction rates for that year would be similarly understated. The *proportions* of the age-specific rates in the total fertility rate, however, may be little affected, since deficient registration is likely to affect all groups equally.

A summary of these rates from 1950 on is given in Table 25. Reading across the table shows clear trends in certain age groups. The decline in fertility since 1950 is shared by all groups, but in quite different proportions; and the proportions themselves follow a consistent pattern, being at their lowest at ages 20–24 and their highest in the oldest group. It is primarily women in the later reproductive ages who have, quite regularly, had fewer children over the years since 1950. The decrease in the rate at ages 20–24 is only 17 per cent – much less than the fall in the gross reproduction rate, so Cypriot women in these ages, most of whose children must be their first, are obviously little affected by overall trends. In the higher groups, however, the decrease amounted to: 25–29, 30 per cent; 30–34, 49 per cent; 35–39, 79 per cent; 40–44, 90 per cent. Of course, these proportions are derived from the data for two particular years, 1950 and 1978, so because age-specific rates vary a little from year to year, the

TABLE 25: AGE-SPECIFIC TOTAL FERTILITY AND GROSS REPRODUCTION RATES IN SELECTED YEARS, 1950–78

Age	Total population		Greek-Cypriots			Turkish-Cypriots
	1950	1960	1965	1973	1978	1978
15–19	29·7	31·5	18·0	17·6	27·0	34·4
20–24	170·2	180·9	157·9	130·2	140·6	144·2
25–29	233·3	207·8	214·2	174·7	163·8	132·8
30–34	171·1	131·7	128·2	92·1	87·9	96·5
35–39	145·5	104·6	82·0	37·3	30·0	32·9
40–44	52·2	31·6	25·9	9·8	5·1	13·7
45–49	9·7	6·5	5·8	1·0	0·3	0·3
TFR	4·06	3·47	3·16	2·31	2·27	2·27
GRR	1·98	1·69	1·54	1·13	1·11	1·11

proportions differ slightly if measured from, say, 1952 to 1979, but no minor variations can conceal the regularity of the pattern. In Cyprus, it is still women of 25–29 years who bear the largest number of children of all quinquennial groups, but whereas their children were greatly in excess of those borne by women aged 20–24 in 1950, that difference had almost disappeared by 1976. In 1950, women over 35 years had 27 per cent of all children born; in 1978, the proportion was only 7 per cent, and child-bearing was virtually confined to a short span in women's lives. Figure 4 illustrates the change which has come about within thirty years.

No comparison of rates in the two main communities in the same year can be made except in 1978, when the sources of the data were necessarily different. However, the rates published in the Turkish-Cypriot *Statistical Yearbook 1978* are of interest in showing – in so far as the data are accurate – that Turkish fertility trends in Cyprus have been remarkably similar to those of the Greek-Cypriots, actually reaching the same low gross reproduction rate of 1·11. We may note, further, the radically different patterns of rates among the Cypriot and mainland Turks: for instance, in Turkey, 23 per cent of all births are to mothers aged

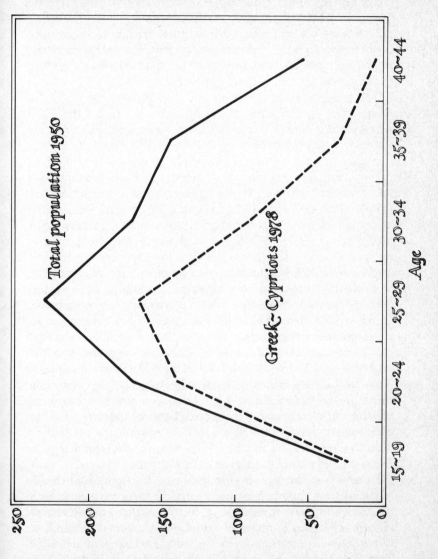

Figure 4. Age-specific fertility rates of total population in 1950 and Greek- Cypriots in 1978.

over 35 (1967), while in Cyprus the equivalent percentage is only 10. These two separate groups of Turks, living forty miles apart, illustrate the United Nations' statement that 'in high fertility countries, women in the early and late periods of the reproductive cycle contribute relatively more to total fertility than do their counterparts in low-fertility countries.[4] Such a contrast between the fertility patterns of sections of the same race living in close geographical proximity must be unusual.

The gross reproduction rate of 2·39 for 1960 calculated by differencing is far from the 1·69 seen in Table 25. Even remembering that it measures performance in the previous fourteen years rather than in 1960 itself and that fertility was falling at the time, it may be implausible. So we now turn to other, perhaps less obvious, factors of relevance. Projecting the age-specific rates back from 1950 suggests a gross reproduction rate in 1946 of about 2·20. This figure, like all the rates shown in Table 25, is derived from vital registration; so because the recording of births up to 1955 (when reported totals were replaced by estimates) was doubtless not wholly complete, they must all err on the low side. And since it is common experience that reporting to a census enumerator the numbers of children born is also deficient but improves in successive censuses, understatement could well have been greater in 1946 than in 1960, resulting in an overestimate of the inter-censal rates. It is, then, likely that the calculated rate of 2·39 for 1946–60 is too high and that the observed $((2·20+1·69)\div 2=)$ 1·94 for about 1954 was too low. Is it reasonable to assume that the true figure lay half-way between them? In the circumstances of Cyprus, the rates based on vital registration were possibly the more reliable of the two series – a conclusion which would not apply in countries with notably defective registration systems. The figure 2·05, applicable to 1954, might be a likely estimate, it now seems.

By applying the age-specific fertility rates derived from differencing to the numbers of women in the appropriate age groups in 1960 and making allowance for the surviving children of women who died in the inter-censal period, a total of 213,319 births between 1946 and 1960 is calculated, implying, on the basis of linear interpolation, a crude birth rate of 29·8 in 1954. This rate, it will be remembered, is probably too high, while the recorded rate for 1954, 26·7, is likely to err on the low side.

178

Between 1960 and 1973 the differencing method gives a gross reproduction rate of 1·24 for the Greek-Cypriot population. As the official figure for 1970 was 1·33, the correspondence between the two independently obtained rates is not unreasonable. In trying to compromise between them, we may note that the official rate resulted from a special exercise to measure the deficiencies in vital registration and so should be comparatively accurate. The true rate may, then, have been about 1·30. Using the age-specific rates obtained by differencing, calculating a crude birth rate for the Greek population mid-way between 1960 and 1973 results in 17·9, applicable to 1966–67 – a much lower figure than the official 22·3 in 1966.

The child/women ratios derived from the censuses may usefully be examined. They are set out in Table 26. The value of such ratios is affected by the quality of the relevant censuses, by varying levels of mortality among young children in the years concerned, and less obviously, by distortions in the age distribu-

TABLE 26: NUMBERS OF CHILDREN AGED 0–4 PER 1,000 FEMALES AGED 15–44, 1891–1973

Census of	Cyprus	Greek Orthodox	Moslem	Urban	Rural
1891	592				
1911	615				
1921	581				
1931	477				
1946	544	542	585		
1960	618	595	692	557	644
1973		382		350	409
Greece					
1940		457			
1971		408		370	465
Turkey					
1950			668		
1960			762		
1970			706		

tion of the female population. The last factor must have had an effect from 1960, because larger proportions of females then aged 15–44 than of young children were then emigrating; as a result, the calculated ratios are higher than they should be. The effect of inaccurate age-reporting in the censuses is less clear, for while Table 26 suggests that fertility in 1960 was at about the same level as in 1891, the age-smoothing process mentioned earlier gives a ratio in 1891 not of 592 but 691. Were that adjustment correct, a clear fall in fertility would be shown. The value of comparisons with other countries such as are given in Table 26 is difficult to assess without detailed knowledge of the enumeration methods used there.

Certain other points in Table 26 may be noted. Fertility was at a higher level among Moslems than the Greek Orthodox, at least from 1940 to 1960, and by 1960 the differential was increasing, so that easily the highest ratio ever recorded in Cyprus was attained by the Moslem population in that year. Further, a similar differential existed between the urban and rural populations, the latter having the higher level. Here, it is noteworthy that in the 1960s the scale of decrease was similar in both areas. The towns led the decline, but the rural population did not lag far behind, once a decline was under way. Between them, these points lead to the speculation that in 1960 the ratio for rural Moslems was probably well over 700.

In comparing Cyprus' rates with those of Greece and Turkey, different points are apparent. One is the marked difference between the levels in the two mainland countries. Was its extent repeated among the Greek and Turkish communities of Cyprus? A glance at Table 26 shows that it was not, Greek fertility being higher in Cyprus than in Greece, while among the Turks it was in Cyprus that the level was lower. Next, fertility did not rise in Greece during and after the Second World War, as it apparently did in Cyprus (and Turkey) – for which the widely differing conditions in the two countries in the 1940s may be thought to account abundantly. The urban–rural differential in the ratio was greater in Greece than in Cyprus – a conclusion to be expected in view of the unusual intermingling of town and country life in Cyprus which was noted earlier.

The balancing equation

Calculating the 'balancing equation' – opening population + natural increase + balance of external migration = closing population – in respect of the inter-censal periods since 1946 serves to indicate whether the elements of growth have been assessed accurately, and may also suggest whether the West or South series of Coale and Demeny's model life tables is the more appropriate to Cyprus.

Using both official data and the numbers of births and deaths arrived at on the basis of mortality levels calculated earlier, together with our estimates of net migration, the equation for 1946–60 is as shown in Table 27. Here, an adjustment to the estimate of net emigration made in Chapter 5 is necessary. Although members of foreign armed services and their families were not reckoned as immigrants or emigrants on arrival or departure (except by mistake, as seems to have happened at least once in the 1950s), 17,600 British were enumerated in the 1960 census,[5] while in 1946 they probably numbered under 1,000. Most of the additions were certainly service men and their families living outside the British bases. They must be reckoned as immigrants for the purposes of the 1946–60 equation, and net migration in this period is therefore reduced from 50–57,000 to

TABLE 27: POPULATION GROWTH ELEMENTS, 1946–60

	West	South	Vital registra-tion data
Enumerated population 1946		450,000	
Enumerated population 1960		573,000	
increase 1946–60 a		123,000	
Births	216,000	223,000	198.000
Deaths	81,000	84,000	51,000
Natural increase b	135,000	139,000	147,000
Migration balance c	−31–37,000	−31–37,000	−31–37,000
a−(b+c)	19–25,000	15–21,000	7–13,000

33–40,000. No such adjustment is necessary for the inter-censal period 1960–73, as it was only after the latter enumeration that most of the service men left Cyprus territory.

Since the equation should balance, we see that of the two models, South gives the better answer. However, the size of the excess in the enumerated population in both is surprising, and it is tempting to accept the equation based on registration data, with its much smaller discrepancy. However, the official average of 3,650 deaths per annum, or 51,000 in the fourteen years, must be inaccurate, we know, since deaths in 1961 were later put officially at 6,200; unquestionably deaths in the 1950s were greatly understated officially. How then did 14,000 to 24,000 extra people come to be found by the later census? In theory, a number of explanations are possible: under-enumeration in 1946; over-enumeration in 1960; an underestimate of inter-censal births; overestimates of inter-censal deaths or emigration; or some combination of them.

The 1946 census probably resulted in some undercount, but hardly by as much as 3·5 to 5·5 per cent, or, more exactly, by that amount more than any deficiency in the 1960 census. That the 1960 enumeration, the first after independence, listed more people than were actually present seems unlikely, since double counting happens rarely, but perhaps mention should be made of the new significance of the numbers of the Greek and Turkish communities to the allocation of seats in parliament and posts in the civil service and police and of a suspicion voiced to the author that the number of the majority community was deliberately exaggerated. However, any such manipulation could lead to inconsistencies within the data, and none have been found; and further, the proportion of Greek-Cypriots in the total indigenous population was actually less, not greater, than in 1946. The totals of births and deaths derive from one base, the Coale and Demeny tables, so if alternative mortality levels were selected, each total would vary, but in the same direction, so that the calculated natural increase would not grow or diminish by very much, certainly not by 15,000. As for migration, perhaps no better estimate than 31,000 to 37,000 net emigrants may be made now, but we should still keep in mind the circumstances from 1947 to 1960 which could just have affected its accuracy – the return of some Cypriots from the war after the 1946 census; civil disturbances; a possibility of unrecorded entry and departure through the British bases. One might guess that Greeks and/or Cypriots found refuge on the island from Greece and from Egypt during those years, but there is little sign of it. Persons born in Turkey were reportedly fewer in 1960 than in 1946. However, it is difficult to avoid a suspicion that the weakest element in the equation is that of migration, even though no evidence to that effect exists. Consultation on the island has not elicited any explanation of the discrepancy, so the equation must be left as it stands – a disappointing outcome to an analysis of population growth at a time when improved statistics should have rendered it easy.

Similar equations for the remaining inter-censal periods – omitting the West version this time – are given in Table 28. In the first equation the official data produce a better result, but here again, it cannot be sound, since deaths in those years too were under-registered. How, then, is the discrepancy of 14,000 accounted for? This time, the reasons seem clear. Firstly, there was an undercount of children, and perhaps older people as well, in 1931. Secondly, Percival remarked that just such a discrepancy was 'understandable in the light of the large numbers of persons, civilian as well as military, who were conveyed to and from the island in vessels or aircraft not subject to normal police formalities'. Together these two points easily account for the apparent excess in the 1946 population. Little comment on the 1960–73 equation is called for in view of the result obtained by using the South tables – although it should be noted that the figures supposedly of the whole population are derived from information supplied by the non-Turkish-Cypriot population only. Ironically some discrepancy is to be expected here, since the first enumeration was conducted *de facto* and the second *de jure*. No *de facto* total in 1973 was recorded, but it was almost certainly less than the enumerated total. Consequently the equation should show an excess in the enumerated population – of, possibly, as much as 10,000, since students abroad were numerous – and for this reason, the answer based on the South tables is less satisfactory than it looks. Finally, it is noteworthy that migration diminished natural growth by about 42 per cent, an exceptional proportion by any standards, not least those of Cyprus herself.

TABLE 28: ELEMENTS OF POPULATION GROWTH, 1931–46 AND 1960–73

	1931–46		1960–73	
	South	Registration data	South	Registration data
Enumerated population 1931, 1960	348,000		573,000	
Enumerated population 1946, 1973	450,000		631,000	
a Increase in population	102,000		58,000	
Births	190,000	183,000	159,000	161,000
Deaths	96,000	79,000	59,000	74,000
b Natural increase	94,000	104,000	100,000	87,000
c Balance of migration	–6,000	–6,000	–42,000	–42,000
a – (*b* + *c*)	14,000	4,000	–	13,000

Age

An example of the effects of smoothing the pre–1946 age data by the formula suggested by the United Nations is given in Table 29. To the series of raw and smoothed totals for 1921 has been added a third distribution derived from the West model life tables and based on life expectancies of 42·5 years for males and 45 years for females and an annual rate of increase of 1·5 per cent. Smoothing eliminates the gross irregularities in the groups over 40, it is noticed, and shows a lower proportion of the population to be aged 30 and over, while more are aged 20–29. Even so, there appear to be real deficiencies in the 20–24 and 25–29 groups:

TABLE 29: 1911 POPULATION BY FIVE-YEAR AGE GROUPS, (a) UNSMOOTHED, (b) SMOOTHED, (c) DISTRIBUTED, ACCORDING TO 'WEST' MODEL STABLE POPULATION LEVEL 11

Age group	Unsmoothed	Smoothed	Distributed by stable population
0–4	36,782	37,897	38,024
5–9	34,127	33,344	32,705
10–14	31,205	30,817	29,621
15–19	25,107	25,538	26,825
20–24	21,448	21,843	24,084
25–29	20,947	20,951	21,480
30–34	19,782	19,277	19,052
35–39	15,738	16,868	16,777
40–44	16,175	15,000	14,651
45–49	11,641	11,557	12,662
50–54	12,597	10,868	10,754
55–59	6,613	8,784	8,861
60–64	9,761	7,770	7,010
65–69	4,178	5,543	5,159
70–74	4,421	4,443	3,433
75 and over	3,586	3,603	3,007
All ages	274,108	274,103	274,105

obviously, emigration is one explanation for them, while another, less obvious, might be the under-enumeration of young migrants *within* Cyprus, as such people, often single, mobile and lodging where they can, are notoriously difficult to enumerate. Smoothing does not, however, serve to reduce the large gap between the numbers aged 15–19 and 20–24, and decreases the even larger gap between the 10–14 and 15–19 groups by only a little. It is here that comparison with the model life table is valuable, because the latter suggests that the census overstated the number aged 10–14 – an unusual feature – while the number aged 14–19 was understated. It also confirms that numerous persons in their twenties escaped enumeration for one reason or another, and goes on to indicate the real pattern of the later age groups.

Other pointers to accuracy in reporting age are found by considering the sex ratios in age groups. Details from selected censuses are given in Table 30. A generally regular pattern is noticeable – more males than females under the age of 15 and between 35 and 50, and more females than males aged 15 to 35. It is yet another indication that the censuses were conducted with consistent, if not perfect, efficiency. Some interesting detail is to be seen. Among older people – for instance the groups 40–44 and 45–49 – the alternating pattern of excesses and deficiencies of males can perhaps be explained by a stronger preference on the part of females for round numbers. It is a point which cannot be proved in the absence of a tabulation by single years of age, but as women's educational standards were lower than those of men, it is at least possible that women knew their ages less accurately and were more prone to declare a round number. The small excess of males in the youngest group was probably genuine, because more male babies are born than females. After the age of 5, however, the pattern is less easy to explain. When ages are not known accurately, it is a common tendency for females to avoid ages between 10 and 20, particularly the adolescent years, and to declare older or younger ages instead, resulting in masculinity ratios below parity from 5 to 9 and from 20 or 25 up to 35. In Cyprus, by contrast, high masculinity ratios were invariably found in the 5–9 group; and, further, a line seemed to exist around age 15, with high ratios immediately below it and low

186

TABLE 30: NUMBERS OF MALES PER 1,000
FEMALES IN AGE GROUPS, 1881–1931

Age group	Census of			
	1881	1901	1921	1931
0–4	1,070	1,046	1,068	1,034
5–9	1,044	1,070	1,014	1,038
10–14	1,131	1,099	1,037	1,064
15–19	925	993	977	947
20–24	938	997	916	939
25–29	988	951	890	871
30–34	886	957	903	931
35–39	1,178	1,209	1,122	1,025
40–44	1,022	993	1,003	905
45–49	1,323	1,178	1,113	1,049
50–54	933	900	978	960
55–59	1,351	1,285	1,254	1,143
60–64	1,004	1,034	1,016	992
65 and over	1,086	1,192	1,070	1,041
All ages	1,037	1,044	1,008	986

ratios above it. While it is not possible to pinpoint the reasons, they probably included the following: (a) some under-enumeration, particularly in the early years, and more particularly of females; (b) biased age reporting in the absence of, specifically, evidence of age, and, generally, of a culture which placed emphasis on age or the year of birth; (c) the emigration of young men, or at least of more young men than young women.

It might be expected that comparing registered births, after allowance is made for early mortality, with the numbers enumerated at appropriate ages in the following census would indicate how accurate the younger recorded age distributions were. Unfortunately, it only serves to show that registration was incomplete. Although the population increased steadily according to the censuses, registered births followed an erratic course; for example, 1921 was the first year in which over 10,000 were recorded, yet almost that number had been registered in 1915, and in the intervening years the totals fell to only 7,800 – 8,100.

Whether such variations were due to the absence of men on war service or to eccentricities in the registration procedure – accumulations of late registrations in particular years, perhaps – is not known now.

Some points about the soundness of more recent age-reporting follow. The problem of obtaining accurate answers to the census question is often met by methods appropriate locally such as placing the year of birth in relation to a well-known event such as flood or a war; or, when practicable, by asking the respondent to consult his birth certificate. As most births were registered by the 1930s, the last device should have been useful to Cyprus' enumerators. What instructions about ascertaining age were actually given to them before 1946 is not known, but the question in that year read 'What was your age at your last birthday?', and went on to guard against the common reluctance to declare age 0 by asking for the month of birth for anyone under one year. The relevant instruction to enumerators was comprehensive: it was of the highest importance that the exact age, not an approximate round figure, should be entered, and persons possessing a birth certificate should be asked to consult it. In 1960 the question asked for month and year of birth, not the age, and the instruction was less exacting: 'If the date of birth is not known, find from the respondent the present age or an estimate of the age.' Thus little responsibility was put on enumerators themselves to ascertain the age accurately. As regards the 1973 and 1976 counts, no information on the point has been given.

Whether age was actually recorded with reasonable accuracy is hard to assess because emigration left irregularities in the normal pattern of ages, but series such as

	1960	1973
10–14	67,102	67,932
15–19	47,658	67,230
20–24	47,082	55,538

are so unusual that some inaccuracy seems likely, particularly because similar eccentricities had not occurred before. The corresponding figures in 1946, for instance, were

10–14	45,848
15–19	43,587
20–24	38,346

It is noteworthy that not only are the figures quoted for 1960 and 1973 inconsistent among themselves, but also that the two patterns lack the resemblance to each other which a consistent bias would have produced. That inaccuracy existed at some points in 1960 is suggested by comparing certain cohorts with 1946. Although the interval was only fourteen years, the comparison is close enough.

1946		1960	
20–24	38,346	35–39	30,803
25–29	32,364	40–44	32,078
30–34	31,029	45–49	26,567
35–39	28,652	50–54	28,284

It is not the amount by which the cohorts diminished which is suspicious – almost any amount could be due to normal mortality plus emigration – but the irregularity of the decrease. However, despite some probable inaccuracy in 1960, there is little doubt that, at all ages over 25, significant numbers of the population were missing, no doubt owing to emigration. Were the model population constructed on a base of persons aged 0–4 numbering the 75,300 actually enumerated, it would total 636,000 instead of the 573,600 found by the census. The difference of 63,000 persons approximates closely to the estimated net emigration between 1921 and 1960 given in Chapter 5.

What appeared to be digit preference was clear in 1960, for instance:

23	8,078	33	6,005	53	3,305
24	9,947	34	9,128	54	9,530
25	8,078	35	5,883	55	3,521

By the time the 20s were reached, more ages ended in 4 than 0 – usually the most popular digit of all – and thereafter more in 4 than any other digit; the 9,530 persons aged 54, for instance, may

189

be compared with 6,248 aged 50, 3,521 aged 55 and 6,648 aged 60. This bias – more pronounced among females, but by no means restricted to them – is something of a mystery. Had the census been taken early in the year, a reported date of birth in 1955 could well have been translated in the census office into age 4, a birth date in 1950 into age 9, and so on – signifying a preference for 0 and 5 in the year of birth which would not have been surprising. However, census day was 11 December. No explanation of the excessive numbers ending in 4 and 9 is, then, apparent, although it is hard to avoid the suspicion that it arose somehow in the process of converting date of birth to age.

Determining age in the youngest years has also presented some difficulty, as these examples of the distribution of ages under 10 show:

Aged	0	1	2	3	4	Total under 5	5–9	Total under 10
1946	124	92	115	103	89	523	477	1,000
1960	107	103	108	103	104	525	475	1,000
1973	94	93	90	97	99	473	527	1,000

As fertility was increasing in 1946, there could have been an unusually large number of infants aged 0, but not 30 per cent more than the number aged 1, so it seems clear that some really aged 1 were reported as 2, or just possibly as 0. The same quirk reappeared in 1960, when, unfortunately, the precaution taken over age 0 in 1946 was not repeated; it is not really likely that the total aged 0 was exceeded by those aged 2 or almost equalled by 5-year-olds. The unusual pattern revealed in 1973 is of a different nature. By then, there probably really were fewer children aged 0–4 than 5–9, owing to the fall in fertility. Further, the distribution among ages 0 to 4 was almost certainly more accurate than previously, although some continued reluctance to declare ages 1 and 2 seems likely.

All such points, it may be added, are not only of importance to an analysis of the age structure, but may also well be significant to the quality in general of the census concerned. Because the problems of ascertaining age correctly are widely known today, the attention, or lack of it, given to them often indicates the degree of care with which the whole census operation is conducted.

The projection

In making the projection described in Chapter 8, the following assumptions were used.

Base population. The population in the government-controlled area as enumerated in 1976 was taken as the base – 495,641 persons. This is not the published total – which was grossed up to include the Turkish-Cypriot population – but a figure which includes some 7,000 persons reckoned to be working temporarily abroad and not actually reported. It is prudent to remember that in 1976 the geographical distribution of the non-Turkish-Cypriot population was quite different from that of earlier years, and that because of this and other factors connected with the 1974 war, the enumeration, conducted *de jure*, may well have omitted a few people or included others wrongly.

Fertility. The averages of the official age-specific fertility rates in 1977–9 were used, viz.:

15–19	26·9
20–24	144·8
25–29	162·5
30–34	89·9
35–39	29·6
40–44	6·0
45–49	0·5

implying a total fertility rate of 2·301, or gross reproduction rate of 1·112 based on the ratio of births of 107 m : 100 f reported in the same years. Although the official numbers of births were estimated, it is likely that the estimates were quite accurate; certainly no better figures can be put forward. A suspicion that estimates are lower than the true figures – because an element of under-registration is usually involved – may be discounted in this case, since in earlier years the official estimates of births were found to have been exaggerated; it is not inconceivable that the same bias occurred in 1977–79. Therefore, while the *pattern* of the age-specific rates is probably good – because neither under-

191

reporting nor weaknesses in the estimation process should have been age-selective – the true total fertility rate could equally have been slightly higher or lower. Whatever its precise level in 1977–79, no other basis exists on which to forecast it in the next two decades. It is already so low that further decline in the future can only be small; on the other hand, its recent fall does not preclude the possibility of some small rise in the future – and, in fact, the official estimate for 1979, 2·387, is higher than for any year since 1972. It appears safest to assume that the level will remain constant in the foreseeable future. Since the age-specific rates in 1977–79 form a pattern already appropriate to a demographically developed society, they also are reckoned to be constant in the projection period.

Mortality.   Similar considerations apply to the future mortality level: minor variations will doubtless occur, but a significant rise cannot be foreseen, and a sizeable fall is impossible. A slight increase in life expectancy over the seventy-one years for males and the seventy-five for females implicit in our calculated mortality level twenty-three in 1970–71 may be achieved at some future time, but whether within the projection period or not cannot be guessed at. The assumption of a constant mortality level twenty-three has therefore been used.

Migration.   Migration in the future is more difficult to assess, because past experience provides little guide to it. Over the last century, emigrants have unquestionably exceeded immigrants, yet it was officially stated just before the 1974 war that that trend was reversed; and since then, returning emigrants – people who left the island in 1974 – may have outnumbered the new emigrants in some years. Taking into account past experience, today's favourable economic situation, the likely inability of agriculture to absorb a much larger labour force in future and the apparently restricted scope for industrial development – not to speak of Cypriots' capacity to settle successfully in other countries – it seems reasonable to assume that emigrants will continue to outnumber immigrants, but perhaps not on the scale of the years since 1945. A net outflow of 1,000 persons per year is therefore assumed, and their distribution by sex and age taken as that of the officially recorded emigrants during the 1970s.

The *component method* has been used, in which the future numbers of males and females in each age group are estimated separately and are then summed to give the total population. The number in each sex-age group who will survive to the next date is arrived at by the application of appropriate mortality rates taken from the South model life tables; the numbers of children to be born are calculated by applying the age-specific fertility rates to the calculated numbers of females in the relevant age groups at each stage of the projection. Calculations have been made in five-year age groups, and at five-year intervals up to the year 2001.

NOTES

1 THE GEOGRAPHICAL AND HISTORICAL BACKGROUND

1 Christodoulou, *The Evolution of the Rural Land Use Pattern in Cyprus*, p. 62.
2 'According to the terms of the convention with the Porte, the island is as completely denuded of money as the summits of the cretaceous hills have been denuded of soil. . . . In the absence of all definite information, no capitalist will embark on any enterprise in Cyprus, which may be ultimately abandoned like Corfu.' Baker, *Cyprus as I Saw It in 1879*, p. 230.

2 THE DEMOGRAPHIC INFORMATION AVAILABLE

1 Lieutenant H. H., later Field-Marshal Lord, Kitchener.
2 A rare, if not unique, occurrence, since it is highly unusual to find even one person directing two consecutive decennial censuses. The author happens to be one such person; outside Cyprus, only one other is known to him.
3 At the time of writing, Volume 1, containing the analysis, is still on sale at the Government Printing Office. Volume 2, containing the tables, is out of print.
4 See the *Statistical Yearbook* for 1978 and 1979.
5 A new publication in 1973. Previously these data were included in the *Demographic Report*.

3 POPULATION GROWTH BEFORE 1878

1 Alastos, *Cyprus in History*, p. 238.
2 D. F. Davidson. Private communication to D. Jenness, author of *The Economics of Cyprus*, p. 40.
3 *Excerpta Cypria*, p. 22.
4 Papadopoullos, *Social and Historical Data on Population (1570–1881)*, p. 38. I am indebted to this work for detail here and elsewhere in this chapter.
5 Vol. IV, p. 17.
6 Detailed in Papadopoullos, *op. cit.*

4 POPULATION GROWTH AFTER 1878

1 Jenness, *The Economics of Cyprus*, p. 103. A more general account of Turkish taxation is given in Baker, *op. cit.*, Chapter XVI.
2 At Larnaca, 'there is shoal water for a distance of about two hundred yards from the shore which causes a violent surf even in a moderate breeze and frequently prevents all communication with the shipping'. At Limassol it was

impossible to land from boats in stormy weather. Baker, *op. cit.*, pp. 17, 257.
3 Bevan, 'Cyprus, Our Newest Colony', p. 264.
4 20 April 1934.
5 Oakden, *Report on the Finances and Economic Resources of Cyprus*, p. 23.
6 Hald, *A Study of the Cyprus Economy*, pp. 44, 48.
7 *Extracts from the First Five-Year Development Plan 1978–82*, p. 1.
8 King, 'North from the Attila Line', p. 124.
9 *News from the North*, 26 December 1979.
10 Bevan, *op. cit.*, p. 268.
11 *Statistical Yearbook 1978*, p. 8.
12 *Special News Bulletin*, 28 January 1975.
13 Percival, 'Some Features of a Peasant Population in the Middle East', p. 196.
14 This tabulation is not included in the *Statistical Yearbook*, but is to be found in *Population Facts* (mimeographed).
15 A figure of 5,000 foreigners, exclusive of armed forces, was mentioned to the author in conversation.
16 V. G. Valaoras, 'A Reconstruction of the Demographic History of Modern Greece', p. 116.

5 MORTALITY, FERTILITY AND MIGRATION

1 *Vital and Migration Statistics 1962*, p. 10. The same work stated that registration of births and deaths since 1900 had been quite reliable.
2 Theodoracopoulos, *The Greek Upheaval*, pp. 55, 89.
3 Minority Rights Group, *Cyprus*, p. 9.
4 Issued by the Progressive Party of the Working People of Cyprus, i.e. the communist party.
5 Minority Rights Group, *op. cit.*, p. 22.
6 Attalides (ed.), *Cyprus Reviewed*, p. 58.
7 Report from the Select Committee on Cyprus, p. 38.
8 By Professor Valaoras, *op. cit.*; and quoted in *Population in Turkey*, p. 29.
9 Shorter, 'Information on Fertility, Mortality and Population Growth in Turkey', p. 6.
10 Valaoras, *op. cit.*, p. 132.
11 *A Ten-Year Programme of Development for Cyprus, 1946*, p. 81.
12 Parliamentary papers, 1879. H. of C. 169, 'Troops and Sickness'.
13 Storrs, *Orientations*, p. 490. Oral statement by the aide-de-camp to the first High Commissioner.
14 Each building sprayed was marked with the date, so that further treatment after a certain interval could be planned. Hence Balfour was able to find in the ruins of Kouklia that the sign 'Temple of Venus' bore the subscription 'DDT 22/2/47'. 'Where the Greeks loved, the British disinfect,' he observed. *The Orphaned Realm*, p. 31.
15 The Director of Medical Services chiefly concerned was Dr R. L. Cheverton. The field work was supervised by Mr Mehmed Aziz, who received the CBE and the award of the Ross Institute for his outstanding services. Mr Aziz has

told the author that at the height of the campaign he had some 700 field
workers in his charge

16 *The Cyprus Review*, March 1950.
17 Personal communication from the office of the Archbishop of Cyprus.
18 The method of estimating emigration used by the author in another country –
projecting the population at one census forward to the next, taking account
of natural increase and immigration, both of which were well documented,
and comparing the result with the population then enumerated – proved
unsuccessful in the case of Cyprus, probably owing to the inaccurate
reporting of ages ('Emigration from Canada in the'1960s').
19 *Statistical Yearbook 1978*, p. 136.

6   OTHER DEMOGRAPHIC CHARACTERISTICS

1 Loizos, *The Greek Gift*, p. 70.
2 Sir R. Palmer, lecture to the Royal Central Asian Society, July 1939.
3 The emigration out of one Mesaoria village, Lefkoniko (Moslem population:
1931 – 142, 1960 – 73), is described in Markides *et al.*, *Lysi*, p. 30.
4 It arrived less than a year later, as a consequence of the 1974 war.
5 Attalides, *Social Change and Urbanisation in Cyprus*, p. 67.
6 Drury, *Western Cyprus: two decades of population upheaval, 1956–76*.
7 Births, marriages and deaths are cross-tabulated by region in the *Statistical
Yearbook*, but as under-registration – unquestionable in the case of deaths,
at least – may not be distributed geographically in proportion to the
population, it would be unwise to assume that these data indicate the
locations of the total population.

7   ECONOMIC ACTIVITY

1 'Economically active' signifies 'furnishing the supply of labour for the
production of economic goods and services during the time reference period
chosen for the investigation'. United Nations, *Principles and Recommendations for the 1970 Population Censuses*, para. 294. For convenience, the
terms 'work', 'worker' and 'labour force' are sometimes used in Chapter 7 in
the same sense.
2 An interesting example is sometimes cited: a domestic servant marries her
employer and so changes from being, formally, economically active (working outside her home) to non-economically active (doing housework at
home), although her activity actually remains the same.
3 United Nations, *op. cit.*, p. 51.
4 Percival's remarks demonstrate the weakness of not defining a reference
period for economic activity, since there is confusion between (a) the concept
of usual activity implicit in the main census questions, and (b) the implication
that people who had spent the summer in building and tourist occupations
and were about to return to farming for the winter could be returned as
unemployed.
5 *The Third Five-Year Plan*, p. 64.
6 *Statistical Yearbook 1978*, Table 82.

8 THE FUTURE

1 *Statistics of Education in Cyprus, School Year 1978–1979.*
2 *World Population Trends and Prospects by Country, 1950–2000.*

APPENDIX

1 Jones, *The Population of Borneo*, p. 83.
2 Smoothing did not, in fact, affect the 1946 age distribution greatly, as Percival showed in his census report (p. 16).
3 The ratio commonly assumed in the absence of precise data. In the last two years for which recorded, not estimated, data were published in Cyprus, 1953–54, the ratio was 104 males: 100 females.
4 *The Determinants and Consequences of Population Trends*, Vol. 1, p. 72.
5 A large majority in Limassol town and suburbs and in Famagusta and Larnaca towns, i.e. near the bases.

BIBLIOGRAPHY

Official Documents

Cyprus *Annual Reports* (under varying titles) 1879–1959

Census Reports (1881, 1891, 1901, 1911, 1921, 1939, 1946, 1960)

Departmental *Annual Reports*

A Ten-Year Programme of Development for Cyprus, 1946 (Nicosia, 1946)

Cyprus Government London Office, *Reports*, 1950s

Department of Statistics and Research, *Cypriot Students Abroad 1977–78*

Department of Statistics and Research, *Demographic Reports*, from 1963

Department of Statistics and Research, *Economic Reports*

Department of Statistics and Research, *Statistics of Education in Cyprus, School Year 1978–79*

Department of Statistics and Research, *Tourism, Migration and Travel Statistics*, from 1973

Department of Statistics and Research, *Vital and Migration Statistics* prior to 1963

Sir R. Oakden, *Report on the Finances and Economic Resources of Cyprus* (London, 1935)

Parliamentary Papers, 1879, H. of C. 169, 'Troops and Sickness'

Planning Bureau, *The Third Five-Year Plan (1972–76)*

Report on Cyprus, based on Information Obtained from Consular Reports, Foreign Office, 1845–77

Report from the Select Committee on Cyprus (London, 1976)

Ed. Sir R. Storrs and B. J. O'Brien, *Handbook of Cyprus* (London, 1928)

B. J. Surridge, *A Survey of Rural Life in Cyprus* (Nicosia, 1930)

Turkish-Cypriot Sources

Extracts from the First Five-Year Development Plan 1978–82

Statistical Yearbook, 1978, 1979

Special News Bulletin (daily)

Other Printed Sources

'A Cinderella Colony', *The Times*, 20 April 1934

D. Alastos, *Cyprus in History* (London, 1955)

M. A. Attalides, *Social Change and Urbanisation in Cyprus* (Nicosia, 1981)

M. A. Attalides (ed.), *Cyprus Reviewed* (Nicosia, 1977)

Sir S. W. Baker, *Cyprus as I Saw It in 1879* (London, 1879)

Patrick Balfour, *The Orphaned Realm* (London, 1951)

William Bevan, 'Cyprus, Our Newest Colony', *United Empire*, London, May 1927

W. Brass, *The Demography of Tropical Africa* (Princeton, 1968)

Demetrios Christodoulou, *The Evolution of the Rural Land Use Pattern in Cyprus* (Bude, England, 1959)

A. J. Coale and P. Demeny, *Regional Model Life Tables and Stable Populations* (Princeton, 1966)

The Cyprus Review, 1942–56

M. P. Drury, *Western Cyprus: two decades of population upheaval, 1956–76* (mimeographed, 1979)

Excerpta Cypria, translated by C. D. Cobham (Cambridge, 1908)

Colonel Fyler, *The Development of Cyprus* (London, about 1899)

Lefkos P. Georgiades, *Some Notes on the Cyprus Economy* (Nicosia, 1953)

Hacettepe University, Institute of Population Studies, *Population in Turkey* (Ankara, 1975)

J. Hajnal, 'Age at Marriage and Proportions Marrying', *Population Studies*, VII (1953), 2

Marjorie W. Hald, *A Study of the Cyprus Economy* (Nicosia, 1968)

Sir G. Hill, *A History of Cyprus* (Cambridge, 1952)

D. Jenness, *The Economics of Cyprus* (Montreal, 1962)

L. W. Jones (L. W. St John-Jones) *The Population of Borneo* (London, 1966)

G. Karouzis, *Report on Aspects of Land Tenure in Cyprus* (Nicosia, 1980)

R. King, 'North from the Attila Line', *Geographical Magazine*, November 1979

R. Hamilton Lang, *Cyprus: its history, its present resources, and future prospects* (London, 1878)

P. Loizos, *The Greek Gift* (Oxford, 1975)

Sir H. Luke, *Cyprus* (London, 1965)

Sir H. Luke, *Cyprus under the Turks, 1571–1878* (Oxford, 1921)

K. C. Markides, E. S. Nikita and A. N. Rangou, *Lysi: social change in a Cypriot village* (Nicosia, 1978)

A. J. Meyer with S. Vassiliou, *The Economy of Cyprus* (Harvard, 1962)

Minority Rights Group, *Cyprus* (London, 1978)

National Academy of Sciences, *Demographic Estimation: a manual on indirect techniques* (Washington D.C.)

R. Oakley, 'Cypriots in Britain', *I Kypros Mas* (1978)

C. W. J. Orr, *Cyprus Under British Rule* (1918)

Sir R. Palmer, 'Cyprus'. Lecture to the Royal Central Asian Society, July 1939

T. Papadopoullos, *Social and Historical Data on Population (1570–1881)* (Nicosia, 1965)

D. A. Percival, 'Some Features of a Peasant Population in the Middle East', *Population Studies*, September 1949

H. D. Purcell, *Cyprus* (London, 1969)

Sir Ronald Ross, *Report on the Prevention of Malaria in Cyprus* (London, 1913)

F. C. Shorter, 'Information on Fertility, Mortality and Population Growth in Turkey', *Population Index*, 34

U. P. Sinha, *Complete Life Tables Based on Coale and Demeny's Model (West) Life Tables* (Bombay, 1972)

Sir R. Storrs, *Orientations* (London, 1945)

L. W. St John-Jones, 'Emigration from Canada in the 1960s', *Population Studies*, XXXIII (1979), 1

B. Stewart, *My Experiences of Cyprus* (London, 1908)

T. Theodoraccpoulos, *The Greek Upheaval* (London, 1976)

United Nations, *the Determinants and Consequences of Population Trends* (1973)

United Nations, *Methods for Population Projections by Sex and Age* (1956)

United Nations, *Principles and Recommendations for the 1970 Population Censuses* (1967)

United Nations, *World Population Trends and Prospects by Country, 1950–2000* (1979)

Vasilios G. Valaoras, 'A Reconstruction of the Demographic History of Modern Greece', *Millbank Memorial Fund Quarterly*, April 1960

Vasilios G. Valaoras, *Urban-Rural Population Dynamics of Greece 1950–1995* (Athens, 1974)

INDEX

Ethnic groups, 30–32, 50–60, 124, 128
Expectation of life, 168

Famagusta, 12, 37, 125, 127
Fertility, 81–91, 171–9; crude birth rates, 81–3; gross reproduction rates, 83–4, 175–9; in Greece, 85, 179–80; in Turkey, 86,
179–80; causes of decline, 86–8; Orthodox Church's attitude
to, 88; Government's attitude to, 89; Greek-Turkish differentials, 90, 165, 173, 180; urban-rural, 90, 165, 173, 180;
age-specific rates, 175–8; total fertility rates, 175–6; in the
future, 191–2
Forestry, 48–9

Greece: population growth, 61; death rates, 68–9; birth rates,
84; age distribution, 114; future population, 161; child/
woman ratios, 179–80
Greek Orthodox community, 51–9
Gross reproduction rates, 83–4, 173, 175–9

Hajnal, J., 119
Harbours, 37
Health conditions, 70–79

Infant deaths, 19–20, 68–70, 77–8, 164–8
Irrigation, 45–7

Land Consolidation Law, 45
Literacy, 86
Locusts eliminated, 41–2
Lusignan period, 11, 26

Malaria, 63, 74–7; eradicated 76–7, 80
Manufacturing, 49–50
Marital status, 115–22
Maronite community, 60
Mechanisation of agriculture, 48
Migration, internal, 14, 39, 108, 110, 121, 126, 128, 130–36
Migration, international, 22–4, 25, 32, 38, 50, 55–7, 91–107,
183, 189; emigration of Moslems, 54–6; totals of emigrants,
91–3; immigration, 92, 105; temporary workers abroad, 95;

destinations of emigrants, 95–7, 99–101; emigration probably understated, 96; characteristics of emigrants, 97; Government's attitude to, 105–6; factor in balancing equation, 182–3; factor in projection, 192
Mining, 39, 49
Mortality: total deaths, 63–5; calculated levels, 65, 162–9; crude death rates, 65–6; in Greece, Turkey, 68–9; exceptional fall in, 79–81; in the future, 192
Moslem community, 54–9
Mother tongue, 51–2

Occupations, 142–8; secondary, 142–3; agricultural, 143–8; changes in, 143–6; by age, 145–6; by religion, 147
Orthodox Church of Cyprus, attitude to family size, 88–9

Percival, D. A., 16, 19, 39, 44, 55, 83, 105, 118, 128, 132, 143, 147, 150, 164, 183
Population estimates: 2nd century BC, 26; Lusignan period, 26; Venetian period, 26; 1572, 27–8; 17th century, 29; 18th century, 30; 19th century, 31
Population growth rates, 34–5, 51–9; projected, 154
Population policy, 89, 160
Projected population, 153, 158–60; growth rates, 154–5; by age, 155; school-going population, 155–7; economically active population, 157; assumptions, 158, 191–2; Turkish-Cypriots, 159–60; methodology, 191–3

Refugees, immigration of, 63, 67, 105
Religion, 19, 87, 88–9, 140
Religion and race, 50–51
Return migration, 103–4, 160
Roads, 36
Rural indebtedness, 13, 43–4

Schooling, future demand for, 155–7
Sex ratios, 108–11, 113, 128, 185
Subdivision of land, 44–5
Survival of children, 162–7

Taxation, 12, 36, 194

Ten Year Development Plan (1946), 13, 39
Terrorist campaigns, 13–14, 20
Total fertility rates, 175–6
Towns, growth of, 124–32, 134
Turkey: population growth, 61; death rates, 68–9; birth rates, 84; age distribution, 115; future population, 161; child/woman ratios, 179–80
Turkish rule (1571–1878), 12, 25, 27–33

Unemployment, 150–52
United Kingdom, immigration from Cyprus, 95–6, 100–103
Urban, definition of, 129
Urban, rural, populations, 125–32; economic activity of, 140

Vital registration, 19–21, 63–5, 82–3, 187

World War I, 13, 38, 86
World War II, 13, 39, 80